The Do-Do Trap
A Christian Guide to Living in the REAL World

Library in the Mafra National Palace, Portugal

By *Emmanuel DeWeg*

~ ※ ~

Copyright Emmanuel DeWeg 2025. Per Acts 4:32, this content may be used at any time, in any way, without compensation, for the glory of Jesus Christ.

A great thanks to the Berean Bible, who has granted all use of their bible verses at no cost: https://berean.Bible/licensing.htm

~ ※ ~

This book is designed and licensed to be photocopied on 8.5" x 11" paper, 2 book pages per side, 4 book pages per piece of paper, a total of 34 papers needed per book.

A free printable version of this book and videos read by the author are available at: EmmanuelDeWeg.org

To provide comments about this edition, to make contributions with unlimited free use, or to subscribe to release information, please go to the publisher's website: EmmanuelDeWeg.org

HB ISBN: 9781640324022
PB ISBN: 9781640324039
Ebook ISBN: 9781640324046
This copy is Edition 1, Revision 1

~ ※ ~

All Greek and Hebrew (H) words are numbered with the Strong and Thayer system for easier research. Biblical quote changes are noted by their [square brackets].

TABLE OF CONTENTS

00. Introduction	4
0. Foundation	5
1. God, Theos 2316	9
2. Is, Eimi 1510	14
3. Love, Agapé 26	17
4. Jesus, Iésous 2424	22
5. Spirit, Pneuma 4151	26
6. The Do-do Trap	30
7. You, Su 4771	35
8. Submission, Hupotassó 5293	41
9. Trinity + You Bread	47
10. Heart, Kardia 2588	50
11. Just in Case	55
12. New, Kainos 2537	56
13. Sin, Hamartia 266	62
14. Excuse, Prophasis 4392	67
15. Light, Phós 5457	74
16. Mature, Teleios 5046	79
17. Humble, Tapeinos 5011	83
18. Word, Logos 3056	88
19. Another, Allélón, 240	95
20. Fruit, Karpos 2590	104
21. Pray, Proseuchomai 4336	109
22. Repent, Metanoeó 3340	117
23. Faith, Pistis 4102	123
24. Pneuma Transform	128
25. Ok, Now What?	133
About the Author	134

00. Introduction

Well, this is an odd book. Greek. Cooking recipes. Maybe even . . . fun?

And you are given the right, even *encouraged,* to copy and distribute without payment to the author, so that you and others may grow more mature in Jesus Christ.

Odd, but that is the book's *point.* The point is to get you stronger in Christ to better live in His love. Isn't that the point of *life?*

To do that, it pays to be *odd.* To *disrupt the familiar.* To make you *think.* You don't have to *agree.* In fact, this author encourages you not to agree.

Why? Well, why do you think?

For *you* to think! 😊 No human communication is perfect. This book will not be either. It could rub you the wrong way. That's OK, as long it drives you to a stronger love union with the Trinity. What is in here can only attempt to lead you to a *glimmer* of the power and glory the Trinity relationship may be in your life.

This author is doing the best he can to communicate the path to that Trinity relationship as little as he knows of it, but the author isn't you. The author can't know *you* like you know *you.* Like God knows *you.*

You are one of a kind among *billions* of humans. Seriously. You are unique. The combination of you and Him, the Trinity + You, will be even more unique. It is up to you to discover *exactly* how to do it for your relationship with Him.

Which is why this book is odd. And repeats ideas in slightly different ways. Hopefully some of these ideas, or *even a single one*, will help your journey to a better relationship with Him. If so — Praise the Lord!

To be successful bringing God's clarity to your life, we must first understand our understandings and define our definitions.

Let us begin. . . .

0. Foundation

What is 'religion' and why do it?

Religion is any ceremonial system we practice to show honor to a greater power, usually done for some gain.

Does religion make life better now or only after we die? Religion *should* make life better now by giving meaning and purpose to 'living'. *Pause and digest — agree, disagree, or discuss?*

Can we mix religions?

No, we can't mix religions. We can't practice two different 'practices' at the same time (like both sailing *and* skiing). Aiming for two different *destinations* leads to neither place. Having different *leaders* also leads to conflict (an ox and horse unequally yoked forever chafe[1]). Therefore, *no*, we can't mix religions to achieve a transformed life. *Pause and digest — agree, disagree, or discuss?*

Is Christianity religion?

In common use the word 'Christianity' is a 'religion', but religion's 'ceremonial practices' *is not* Christianity. Being a Christian means you are a disciple of Jesus Christ. Jesus Christ is not a ceremony. He is a *person* to have a relationship. The source of *His* changes *in you* comes from knowing *His love for you*.

Why is Christianity THE WAY?

1. *Stable central message:* Christianity captures Christian principles **from Jesus**, the actual leader.
2. *Key points of truth:* Christian disciple's abuse and martyrdom **without gain** show belief that comes only from truth.
3. *Greatest verification:* Only Christianity allows, is bombarded by, and **passes verification**.
4. *Results:* Father, Son, and Holy Spirit, have **improved more lives** than any other religion.

---

[1] 2 Corinthians 6:14 "Do not be unequally yoked with unbelievers. For what partnership can righteousness have with wickedness? Or what fellowship does light have with darkness?"

Pause and digest — agree, disagree, or discuss?

Are all Christians the same?

1. *Same* body, same physical and spiritual needs (food and love).
2. *Different* DNA, different experiences (nature and nurture), and different passions. Each is special to God.
3. *Different* definitions and application of world view (how we communicate and see the world).
4. *Same* body of Christ (the hands aren't more important than the feet).[2]
5. *Results:* Christians are both the same and different depending on what trait we are comparing and how we measure.

Pause and digest — agree, disagree, or discuss?

Are all churches the same?

1. *Same* Greek sourced Bible, same leader (Christ).
2. *Different* DNA, different experiences (nature and nurture), different ways to worship.
3. *Different* definitions and application of world view (how we communicate and see the world).
4. *Same* body of Christ (the hands aren't more important than the feet).
5. *Results:* Churches are both the same and different depending on what trait we are comparing and how we measure.

Pause and digest — agree, disagree, or discuss?

What identifies non-Christ church participants?

1. Does evil while hiding behind the name of 'good' (like hiding behind the name of Christ or 'Christian').
2. Has secrets.
3. Uses a special Bible, has unique interpretations, claims privileged insights, or new revelations.[3]
4. Leaders benefit in non-Christ ways.

Pause and digest — agree, disagree, or discuss?

---

[2] 1 Corinthians 12:14 "For the body does not consist of one part, but of many."

[3] Revelation 22:18 "I testify to everyone who hears the words of prophecy in this book: If anyone adds to them, God will add to him the plagues described in this book."

What is true Christianity?

'Love God and love others,' fulfills and supersedes text rules.[4]
1. God's love relationship with us,
2. changes us,
3. and enables us to love others through relationship.

GOD → Love Relationship → Us → Love Relationship → Others

Pause and digest — agree, disagree, or discuss?

What is sin?

God = Love (1 John 4:16[5])
Sin = Not-God (1 John 3:5[6])
Sin = Not-Love

Sin is when we *not-love* (which is a very broad definition). But we don't need to focus on sin *avoidance* to live best, we need to focus on God *experience*! (More on this later.) *Pause and digest — agree, disagree, or discuss?*

How then shall we live?

God is Love,
Submit to *His* love, so that
You can love others
As you and they are able
As He loves you.

What does this submissive but relational love look like? How much should we ask God for help to be more fruitful in the Spirit?[7] How often should we listen for an answer? How thankful should we be for peace, help, and answered prayers? How should we keep loving, fruitful boundaries? (More on these later.) The answers are always found in that specific moment from our relationship with God.

---

[4] Galatians 5:14 "For the entire Law is fulfilled in this one word: 'You shall love your neighbor as yourself.'"

[5] 1 John 4:16 "And we have come to know and believe the love that God has for us. God is love; whoever abides in love abides in God, and God in him."

[6] 1 John 3:5 "And you know that He appeared, so that He might take away sins; and in Him there is no sin."

[7] Galatians 5:22-23 "But the fruit of the Spirit is love, joy, peace, patience, kindness, goodness, faithfulness, gentleness, self-control. Against such things there is no law."

Or put a different way:
1. Relationship with God,
>> leads to
2. Identity in God,
>> leads to
3. Becoming of God.

Usually Christian focus is on *becoming* (#3 as in 'doing good'), but we can't securely transform without #1 and #2 because skipping to #3 means we're doing everything with our *own* power in *our* way to *our* idea of good.

The Trinity (God the Father, Jesus the Son, and the Holy Spirit) is an unlimited source of power who knows the real best way to do the best good. What is the point of being a Christian if we're going to do it ourselves without Christ? That is not a relationship. The Trinity + You *is* a relationship that transforms.

Mature in Christ

We must not be a Christian by ourselves. We must be a Christian *in Christ*.[8] To be 'in Christ' means maturing in the Trinity + You relationship. A strong relationship requires us to understand our understanding. Who do we think God is? What does He want for us? What is holding us back? How much does God *really* love us?

As you go through each chapter that tries to answer these questions, ask yourself, "How can I apply this to live a fuller life in Jesus Christ?"

A prayer from Ephesian 1:18-19

I ask that the eyes of your heart may be enlightened, so that you may know the hope of His calling, the riches of His glorious inheritance in the saints, and the surpassing greatness of His power to us who believe.

---

[8] Romans 6:23 "For the wages of sin is death, but the gift of God is eternal life in Christ Jesus our Lord."

1. God, Theos 2316

Who is God? Is He like Santa, mysteriously giving gifts? Or like your human parents, imperfect or worse? Is God someone watching with a lightning bolt to zap your every mistake? Or a flower toting hippie saying, 'Love, love, love,' all the time? Or a sadist, causing pain and misery, 'for your good'?

Where would you place your main view of who is God?

▲ Anger   ▲ Love

High Level

Our view of God can come from many places: parents, teachers, culture, and more. Are those views true to *the Bible* and our experience of God? Can God be 'punisher', 'gift giving Santa', and other things all at the same time without conflict? If there is conflict in His identity, how is that resolved? What are *your* biggest stumbling blocks to know and experience *the true God*? How does this affect your relationship to God, your Christian fruit, and your relationships to others? *Pause and digest — agree, disagree, or discuss?*

The Bible and Christian life experience shows us the three parts of one God: Father, Jesus, and Holy Spirit. If we were to make a *typical* definition of the parts of God, it would be easy to argue in the Bible that the Father is wrath (Old Testament), Jesus is love (New Testament), and the Holy Spirit is . . . better not talked about.

But that isn't true! God is one! From the Old Testament, "the LORD is One,"[1] through the New Testament, "God is one,"[2] God *directly* shows He is of one spirit, one mind, and one intent in these verses and elsewhere.

God tells us His one intent. It is relationship with *you.*

> "I have given them the glory You gave Me, <u>so that they may be one</u> as We are one." — John 17:22

---

[1] Deuteronomy 6:4 "Hear, O Israel: The LORD our God, the LORD is One."
[2] James 2:19 "You believe that God is one. Good for you! Even the demons believe that — and shudder."

If God is one, and being Christian means being one with Him, we must therefore define, "Who is God?" to define, "who am I?" *Pause and digest — agree, disagree, or discuss?*

God is too great to fully understand[3] so we must first accept knowing only what we are able. Fortunately, God made it easy. First John 4:16 tells us directly "God is love." And of the 78 times the phrase "endures forever" is in the Bible, usually it is talking about God's "*love* endures forever"[4] (*not* wrath or anger!).

God is Love

God is love. The Bible tells us so. God's actions are that of a *loving* God. We see God's love for you spans the Old and New Testament, from Deuteronomy 23:5, "God loves you,"[5] to Revelation 1:5, "God loves you."[6] *Pause and digest — agree, disagree, or discuss?*

Some might disagree that "God is love" by asking about the "wrath of God." If "God is love," how can there be "wrath" (specifically against me!)? The question is misleading because our understandings of these words, our one-dimensional view of God Himself, and the full situations where God's actions occurred. God doesn't have "wrath" against His children,[7] but against *ungodliness*![8]

First, there are progressions of God's salvation plan and presence in the world, but His fight against ungodliness is the same.[9] The people of Gomorrah were very different than Abraham's Canaan, which were different than Jerusalem when Jesus walked. People today can't understand any of these cultures, or do they track God's progression of salvation plans, so can't judge what is 'nice' from our cushy and safe armchairs today. Still, God wants "none to perish."[10] He has no pleasure

---

[3] Job 9:10 "He does great things beyond searching out, and wonders without number."

[4] Psalm 136, 2 Chronicles 7:3, and more, both New and Old Testament.

[5] Deuteronomy 23:5 "Yet the LORD your God would not listen to Balaam, and the LORD your God turned the curse into a blessing for you, because the LORD your God loves you."

[6] Revelation 1:5 "To Him who loves us and has released us from our sins by His blood, . . ."

[7] 1 Thessalonians 5:9 "For God has not appointed us to suffer wrath, but to obtain salvation through our Lord Jesus Christ."

[8] Romans 1:18 "For *the* wrath of God is revealed from heaven upon all ungodliness and unrighteousness of men, suppressing the truth by unrighteousness, . . ."

[9] Romans 1:32 "Although they know God's righteous decree that those who do such things are worthy of death, they not only continue to do these things, but also approve of those who practice them."

[10] 2 Peter 3:9 "The Lord is not slow in keeping His promise as some understand

in their deaths.[11] In other words, *God never enjoys your pain!* If you have conflict with this image of "God is love", though there are a pile of verses to support it, ask yourself, "Why do I have conflict?" *Pause and digest — agree, disagree, or discuss?*

Next, when we read, "God is love," it does not mean that God's actions are pleasant. God can exhibit many actions *through* love. When people challenge God by saying, "He must not be all powerful because if He was, He would have done this or that . . ." the answer is that God had a *good* reason for when and how He acted, that *we* simply don't understand, can't understand, or have the wrong expectations ('God, I want my grandma to live to 150'). *Pause and digest — agree, disagree, or discuss?*

> **God; θεός; Theos:**
> Strong's 2316. THE Divinity. The only and true God, creator of all things, sustainer of all things. Used 1327 times in the New Testament. Research also "Father" (patér 3962).

Would a doctor have 'love' or 'wrath' for the sickness that was killing his patient? Would that doctor be 'mean' cutting off a finger if it saved the patient's life? Likewise, is it ok for *us* to be angry about evil? Why not God? Should we let a neighbor be robbed, or should we try to stop it? What if *we* were being robbed? Which of these actions show we are "loving our neighbor"? Are we allowed to be angry about the invasion of evil? Of course we are! We are in a spiritual battle[12] where 'good' and 'bad' have been written on our hearts.[13] If we can have righteous anger, why not God? *Pause and digest — agree, disagree, or discuss?*

The key here is that God *is* love and *acts through* love. Only when we start from this framework, can we truly *trust* God. God's *love* for others removed the evil of Sodom and Gomorrah.[14] If you don't believe this was 'good', imagine your family living there!

---

slowness, but is patient with you, not wanting anyone to perish but everyone to come to repentance."

[11] Ezekiel 33:11 "Say to them: 'As surely as I live, declares the Lord GOD, I take no pleasure in the death of the wicked, but rather that the wicked should turn from their ways and live. Turn! Turn from your evil ways! For why should you die, O house of Israel?'"

[12] Ephesians 6:12 "For our struggle is not against flesh and blood, but against the rulers, against the authorities, against the powers of this world's darkness, and against the spiritual forces of evil in the heavenly realms."

[13] Hebrews 10:16 "This is the covenant I will make with them after those days, declares the Lord. I will put My laws in their hearts and inscribe them on their minds."

[14] Genesis 18:20 "Then the LORD said, "The outcry against Sodom and Gomorrah

Finally, we must also be careful to avoid assigning to God the result of physics or man's free-choice action. A drunk driver must own *their own* consequences, and we should put the fault there, not on God. In Daniel 5:26,[15] God counted the end of King Belshazzar's days, but the King was too lazy to protect his gates.[16] Was this God's 'wrath' or natural consequences?

If we drink poison, remain in the path of the hurricane, or overspend our budget, would the results be God's 'wrath' or natural consequences? God tells us, "the wages of 'not-love' is death."[17] Why then are we surprised when bad stuff happens caused by the free-choice of ourselves or others? Did the people in the Bible lose 'God's favor' or did they take their eyes off of God[18] and their lives reflected that? *Pause and digest — agree, disagree, or discuss?*

Resistance

People's *resistance* to accepting the idea that "God is love" may be a result of their own life experiences.[19] A tree with 1,000 cuts does not flourish. So too a child receiving 1,000 insults from their parents or other relationships does not flourish. How can such a child grow up under these circumstances understand or accept that "God is love", when most of their experience is not-love, conditional-love, or have to feed these people's self-love? Do *we* fully accept God's love? *Pause and digest — agree, disagree, or discuss?*

God is <u>one</u>, therefore we can experience Jesus or the Holy Spirit and *know* God.[20] Jesus openly *loved* those that sought Him; children,[21] seekers,[22] and those that suffer.[23] Jesus was *angered* by those that

---

is great. Because their sin is so grievous . . ."

[15] Daniel 5:26 "And this is the interpretation of the message: MENE means that God has numbered the days of your reign and brought it to an end."

[16] Proverbs 12:24 "The hand of the diligent will rule, but laziness ends in forced labor."

[17] Romans 6:23 "For the wages of sin is death, but the gift of God is eternal life in Christ Jesus our Lord."

[18] John 3:14 "Just as Moses lifted up the snake in the wilderness, so the Son of Man must be lifted up."

[19] Ecclesiastes 1:13 "What a heavy burden God has laid upon the sons of men to occupy them!"

[20] John 14:9 "Anyone who has seen Me has seen the Father."

[21] Matthew 19:14 "But Jesus said, 'Let the little children come to Me, and do not hinder them! For the kingdom of heaven belongs to such as these.'"

[22] Mark 10:21 "Jesus looked at him, loved him, . . ."

[23] Luke 19:41 "As Jesus approached Jerusalem and saw the city, He wept over it."

promoted not-love in the name of God; profiteers[24] and hypocrites.[25] To be the best disciple, we must do as God commands, and let ourselves *be* loved *to* love others:

> *"As I have loved you, so you also should love one another."*
> *— John 13:34*

Pause and digest — agree, disagree, or discuss?

What is the Theme?

God is Love,
Seek and Submit to His love.
to love one another.

---

[24] John 2:16 "To those selling doves He said, 'Get these out of here! How dare you turn My Father's house into a marketplace!'"

[25] Luke 13:15 "'You hypocrites!' the Lord replied. 'Does not each of you on the Sabbath untie his ox or donkey from the stall and lead it to water?'"

2. Is, Eimi 1510

"What is truth?" Pontus Pilate asks,[1] and so should we. People claim to know "What is truth" about God, about what is 'good', what the Bible 'says', and what is 'right'. But what "is truth"? Does this mean the same truth all the time or is it relative, something you can decide yourself? How much is your maturing in Christ held back by your trust of God's "truth"?

Where would you place your view of God's truth?

▲ Relative   ▲ Fixed

High Level

You wouldn't sit on a chair without trusting that it was there, *fixed*, solid and dependable. It also makes sense to only depend on a God that is fixed, in a fixed world, with a fixed truth.

The Lies

Yet the Liar hurls deceptions to obstruct your relationship with God. Lies like:
1. All truth is relative.
2. All paths lead to the right places.
3. *You* decide what is 'truth'.
4. The map (Bible) is filled with mistakes and lies.

Which are all great ways to get lost on a road trip or in life. *Pause and digest — agree, disagree, or discuss?*

The Truth

If all truth is relative (#1), how does one build a house, buy a car, or make a sandwich? "Kids, instead of Disneyland, we're going to the dump, it's all the relative . . ." One couldn't apply 'all truth is relative'

---

[1] John 18:38 "Pilate says to Him, 'What is truth?' And having said this, he went out again to the Jews and says to them, 'I find no guilt in Him.'"

to physical life, so it is logical to keep it away from spiritual life. There must be one fixed truth.

If all paths lead to right places (#2), or, 'there are many paths up the mountain', this assumes that dead ends aren't fatal, all paths have the same end points, and *the messenger of this lie is correct.* What if there are many paths, that go many places, and the messenger wants you lost? One would hope this lie would be tested before betting our life on it. There must be one right place, and one path to get there.

If every individual gets to decide for themselves 'the truth' (#3), then we now have 8.3 billion people and 'truths' in the world. Every evil in the world is also 'truth', and there can be no fixed 'good'. Both of these statements make this lie

> **Is; εἰμί; eimi:**
> Strong's 1510. To be, exist, 'is', or 'am'. "God is love" could be "God *am* love," (same eimi) signifying *He* is our definition of love. Eimi is key to expanding our understanding of pivotal verses such as, "I AM," of Exodus 3:14, to the seven times Jesus says, "I am" in John, to "Who do you say *I am*?" in Matthew 16:15.

impossible to depend on to transform our lives. There must be one truth, and one creator of that truth, else there would be *chaos* in everything and everywhere, regardless if we were defining gravity or kindness.

If that map was filled with mistakes (#4), it matters *only if the mistakes are substantial.* One doesn't toss out the steak if it falls in the coals, nor get rid of the map if a new road has been built. Our map, the Bible, is stable enough, true enough, that even if there have been errors in a few verses (which this author believes there are only variants but not errors),[2] the Bible's <u>message</u> is redundant enough to depend on God with it: "God loves you and wants a relationship with you to transform you and those around you with His love" (— why do people fight against Love?). *Pause and digest — agree, disagree, or discuss?*

These four lies make an easy excuse to those *who want to avoid submission* to God. These lies seem *just truthful enough* to plant doubt in those wanting to have a stronger relationship with God. These lies fracture the foundation of Christians enough that they resort to old, fleshly habits when life gets tough.[3]

The result is a less powerful, less God filled life.

---

[2] Basic proofs are provided in *Reader's Digest The Bible Through the Ages* ISBN 9780895778727, Josh McDowell's *Evidence That Demands a Verdict,* and Lee Strobel's *The Case for Christ.* Or search online about 'Bible variants are not errors'.

[3] Matthew 13:21 "But since he has no root, he remains for only a season. When trouble or persecution comes because of the word, he quickly falls away."

One Must Choose: Believe God or Not

There is a fixed truth that frames both Testaments: love. Be it for God, your neighbor, or yourself — love. Trusting that God acts through love removes all conflicts in the Bible.

God loves you. He breathed life into you.[4] This truth is fixed and unchanging. God loves you. You can depend on this truth *totally* even if *you can't* touch or understand *all* of God. It does not matter if the Bible had a comma changed from the original Greek, or the events are told from different perspectives, or who wrote the book of Hebrews — *God loves you*.

We must *choose* to believe God regardless of the lies trying to distract us so that we may have the power of God's relationship to transform our lives — today! *Pause and digest — agree, disagree, or discuss?*

What then is the "gospel", which translates to "good news"? It is that God has made a way to have a relationship with Him, through Jesus Christ and the Holy Spirit, by you submitting to His truth.

God, Jesus, and the Holy Spirit are *one*.[5] They want to relate to you as the Trinity + You. This relationship of love, pours love into you, and spills out to others.

What is the Key Takeaway?

God's love for you is a fixed truth.
Submit to His love, so that
You can love others.

---

[4] Job 33:4 "The Spirit of God hath made me, and the breath of the Almighty hath given me life."

[5] Mark 14:62 "And Jesus said, 'I am (eimi 1510). And you will see the Son of Man sitting at the right hand of Power and coming with the clouds of heaven.'"

3. Love, Agapé 26

"God is love."[1] *Love is the one attribute that frames both the New and Old Testament. If we want to relate to God and experience His fullness in our hearts,*[2] *we need to figure out what 'love' means to God.*

The Greek relationship word 'agapé', which today is usually labeled as 'love' appears 116 times in the New Testament. The object of that relational love, 'beloved' (agapētoi) appears 61 times. 'Love' is obviously important. But what is 'love'?

Where would you place your definition of what love is about?

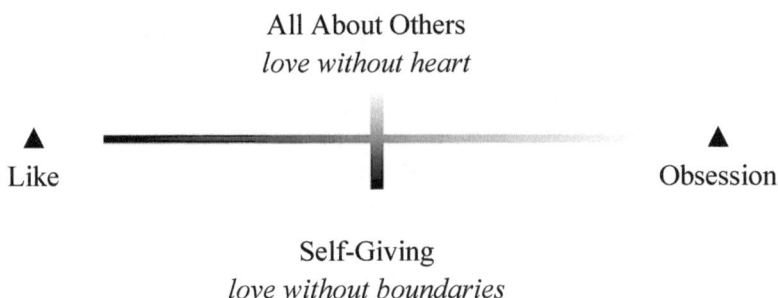

High Level

Left to right, does 'love' indicate 'liking', or is it expressed more in an 'obsession' way? Top to bottom, is 'love' checking the box about what you have done for 'others', or more like the bottom self-giving and how much others take from you? Are these 'human-love' types totally off from God's love?

Do you *mean* the same when you say, "I love peanut butter," "I love my spouse," and "I love my dog"? I hope not! This author's hope is your relationship to all three is *very* different, yet we use the *same* word each time, 'love'. How many difficulties are caused by people using the same words, with different understandings of those words? *Pause and digest — agree, disagree, or discuss?*

---

[1] 1 John 4:8 "Whoever does not love does not know God, because God is love."
[2] Romans 5:5 "And hope does not disappoint us, because God has poured out His love into our hearts through the Holy Spirit, whom He has given us."

Different Definitions Produce Discord

Important here as always is to stick to *God's definition*, which needs to work for *all* examples in the Bible. The definition of 'love' must work for both loving God and loving our neighbor.[3]

Here is this author's definition of love: *charity* and *goodwill* (which is how the King James Bible translated agapé). How are charity and goodwill then defined? God and Jesus and the Holy Spirit are one, so if you know one, you know them all.[4] Therefore, God is love, love is charity and goodwill, and charity and goodwill are *inherent* in the fruit of the Spirit: "love, joy, peace, patience, kindness, goodness, faithfulness, gentleness, and self-control."[5] If these definitions seem redundant, they are, trying to get *limited* humans to understand an *infinite* God. *Pause and digest — agree, disagree, or discuss?*

> **Love; ἀγάπη; agape:**
> Strong's 26. Derived from the verb, "to love," agapé is a chosen *state of being* that leads to action. Besides charity and goodwill, synonyms could include affection, benevolence, esteem, or in verb form wish well, longing, or desire kindness upon.

The author would put his definition of 'love' in the middle of the graph, but would *move it* depending on the situation and what the author thinks God's desire is 'right' in that moment. Goodwill and charity are important for all relationship interactions, but their breadth and depth are different depending on which two parties are involved.

Seem unclear? For sure. It is unclear because *rule-based* living can't apply to all situations, but *love can*! Everything in a God filled life *depends on love.*[6]

With these multiple expressions defining 'love', how should one know which to use *in the moment?* God tells us to use our free-choice discretion,[7] guided by the Bible[8] and ask the Holy Spirit what to do *in*

---

[3] Matthew 22:37, 39 "Jesus declared, 'Love the Lord your God with all your heart and with all your soul and with all your mind.'" . . . "And the second is like it: 'Love your neighbor as yourself.'"

[4] 1 John 5:8 ". . . the Spirit and the water and the blood--and these are three in one."

[5] Galatians 5:22-23 "But the fruit of the Spirit is love, joy, peace, patience, kindness, goodness, faithfulness, gentleness, self-control. Against such things there is no law."

[6] Matthew 22:40 "All the Law and the Prophets hang on these two commandments."

[7] Proverbs 2:11 "Discretion will watch over you, and understanding will guard you, . . ."

[8] 2 Timothy 3:16 "All Scripture is God-breathed and is useful for instruction, for conviction, for correction, and for training in righteousness, . . ."

the moment[9] to produce good fruit.[10] As we grow, the more our free-choice is in union as the Trinity + You, the more *our* discretion becomes one with *His* — isn't that a good goal, to 'live in Christ'? *Pause and digest — agree, disagree, or discuss?*

Test Cases

Here are some verses to test the definition of *agapé* and put 'love' into practice.

1. "<u>Love</u> the Lord your God with all your heart and with all your soul and with all your mind and with all your strength." (Mark 12:30) — This is the ultimate love, a goodwill and charity *obsession* with God first, and alignment to Him in all that we do. He is the creator of all! This verse appears also in Deuteronomy 6:5, though in the New Testament Jesus includes the "mind" which this author feels is another indicator to use our discretion.

2. "<u>Love</u> your neighbor as yourself." (Mark 12:31) — Having 'goodwill' to our neighbor is a lot easier to understand than 'love'. Mark 12:31 is the same verse as Leviticus 19:18, where the Hebrew word for love means 'affection', which is very similar to 'goodwill' and 'charity'. Note that some people aren't very kind to themselves, so have 'goodwill' for yourself too! How does this work in practice? Simply be kind without being insistent: sharing a hello or cookies, keep the peace, and forgive petty slights.[11]

3. "But I tell you, <u>love</u> your enemies and pray for those who persecute you, . . ." (Matthew 5:44) — Can we have 'goodwill' towards our enemies and pray for their redemption in Christ? Absolutely. We may not feel able, though this is God's perfect 'goodwill', and so we can ask God to help us be able.[12]

---

[9] Luke 11:13 ". . . how much more will your Father in heaven give the Holy Spirit to those who ask Him!"

[10] Matthew 7:17 "Likewise, every good tree bears good fruit, but a bad tree bears bad fruit."

[11] Leviticus 19:18 "Do not seek revenge or bear a grudge against any of your people, but love your neighbor as yourself. I am the LORD."

[12] In *Tramp for the Lord* by Corrie Ten Boom, Chapter 7 *Love Your Enemy*, she describes the amazing power of asking God for help to provide the 'goodwill'.

With these first three verses giving examples, we see that for love to produce 'good fruit', it must have different depth of expression and boundaries in each relationship. Handing someone $20 to do damage to themselves is *not* love, nor is giving your pearls to pigs,[13] nor is it 'love' to do other acts of 'goodwill' that promotes the 'world'.[14] In other words, 'love' thy neighbor has limits![15] *Pause and digest — agree, disagree, or discuss?*

> 4. God so <u>loved</u> you, (yes, you specifically!) that He created a way to give Himself to you. That whoever accepts this gift shall have an eternal relationship with God. (John 3:16) — But many people leave their gift unopened! Or they open it and wait for death (also known as 'mansion moving day'[16]). God didn't provide the Holy Spirit *now* to wait for a relationship with you at your physical death. He wants to relate with you *now* as the Trinity + You! *Pause and digest — agree, disagree, or discuss?*

God Wants a Relationship with You — *Now!*

God loved you before you accepted his gift of Jesus Christ. He loved you even though you may not have wanted a relationship with Him.

Now that you have accepted His gift, part of that acceptance is to live your life through Him, which means maturing your love relationship *with Him*, in a Trinity + You union. As you mature, your love for God will move on the graph from *like* to *obsession* as you understand more about Him and yourself.

Strong love relationships require *real* interactions based on trust (faith) and accountability (good fruit). One can't have a love relationship to peanut butter, even though we say, "I *love* peanut butter." One *can* only have love relationships (goodwill and charity relationships) to *others*. Even if the relationships are lopsided in love

---

[13] Matthew 7:6 "Do not give dogs what is holy; do not throw your pearls before swine. If you do, they may trample them under their feet, and then turn and tear you to pieces."

[14] 1 John 2:15 "Do not love the world or anything in the world. If anyone loves the world, the love of the Father is not in him."

[15] Proverbs 25:17 "Seldom set foot in your neighbor's house, lest he grow weary and hate you."

[16] John 14:2 "In My Father's house there are many mansions. And if not so, would I have told you that I go to prepare a place for you?"

quantity (God/us, parent/child, or invalid/caretaker relationship), they can still be strong *love* (charity and goodwill) relationships.

A strong love relationship is not about do-do action, it is about *love*. There are those who do the right 'action' without love, goodwill, or charity, but these interactions are unsettling: such as inviting you to the group (to make our numbers grow) or sending you gifts (but never talking to you). You *can't* have a stronger relationship with these people as there is no love, goodwill, or charity. Paul calls these unsettling experiences "clanging cymbals",[17] as everything *seems* right, but *is* jarringly wrong.

The Point

Here is the point of the Old and New Testament: God wants a relationship with you, a real agapé-love-goodwill-charity relationship union as the Trinity + You. Seen from this perspective, the Bible makes sense, the battle of good and evil in this world makes sense, and our purpose (growing more in union with the Trinity) makes sense.

Insert your name in John 3:16 to see how powerfully true it is that God wants a relationship with you:

God so loved you Olivia, Mary, Mia, . . . God so loved you Liam, Matthew, Mateo, . . . That He sent His only son, Jesus, to bring you to Him, to have an everlasting relationship with you. (starting now!)

Good news! Good news! The more open and honest relationship we have with God, through reading, listening, and submitting to Him, the more we can understand God's love for us, know *who we truly are* and were created by Him *to be*. By being in that love relationship, by being more *in union* with Him,[18] we express more *of Him*, to produce the most 'good fruit' of all![19] *Pause and digest — agree, disagree, or discuss?*

What is the Key Takeaway?

Submit to God's love, so that
You can love others,
And know what 'love' means.

---

[17] 1 Corinthians 13:1 "If I speak in the tongues of men and of angels, but have not love, I am only a ringing gong or a clanging cymbal."

[18] 1 John 2:6 "Whoever claims to abide in Him must walk as Jesus walked."

[19] John 15:5 "I am the vine and you are the branches. The one who remains in Me, and I in him, will bear much fruit. For apart from Me you can do nothing."

4. Jesus, Iésous 2424

What is it about Jesus Christ? Love Him, ignore Him, hate Him — only Jesus Christ is the recipient of such strong opinions worldwide. What causes that? Who and what was and is Jesus Christ?

Where would you place your definition of Jesus Christ?

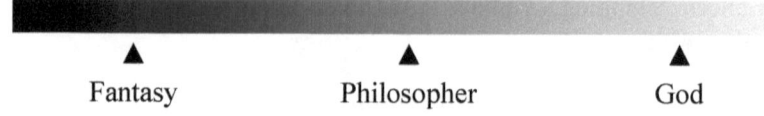

    Fantasy   Philosopher   God

Life of Jesus

About 2025 years ago, a baby was born to a poor traveling couple. The baby (Jesus) grew up in the typical small town Jewish life, with a few memorable events.

When Jesus was about 30 years old, He went into religious teaching full time, telling people to "give up your jobs to follow Me," to learn to be teachers with a following too.[1]

Incredible tales were told of Jesus, all exhibiting a love for God: demanding purity in God's worship center, feeding and healing thousands of people, teaching that "love" is the greatest command.[2]

City after city where Jesus went, the religious authority found fault with Jesus because He didn't follow the 'rules', do the 'rituals', and do all that stuff people were 'supposed to do' to be 'right'. The question was, *who* was the religious authority 'right' with? And did all that do-do-do help them be-be-be more of God? *Pause and digest — agree, disagree, or discuss?*

And Then

The religious authority complained so much, that Jesus was executed by the government. This should have been the end of Jesus and His teachings. But people started seeing Him, talking with Him, and even ate with Him. This wasn't a rare thing. It went on for 40 days and

---

[1] Matthew 4:19 "'Come, follow Me,' Jesus said, 'and I will make you fishers of men.'"
[2] John 15:17 "This is My command to you: Love one another." Also Matthew 22:36-40 and Mark 12:28-31.

with more than 500 people.³ And then He wasn't seen or heard from after that, except by a guy that was trying to kill followers of the Jesus "Way".⁴

The followers of Jesus wrote down what they saw Him do and say, and how people could then "live in" Jesus.⁵ No one could change what these followers said about Jesus, even to the point of being whipped, stoned, jailed, or executed.⁶

These followers were successful spreading the teaching of Jesus Christ so that today more than half the world knows His name.⁷ Unfortunately the definition of "Jesus" varies, *a lot. Pause and digest — agree, disagree, or discuss?*

Debate

Who and what was and is Jesus Christ? Is Jesus even real? Yes, Jesus existed. Jesus and his followers were referenced by contemporary non-believers Josephus, Tacitus, Pliny, and Suetonius. Therefore, *somebody* at that time named Jesus was walking around teaching people and making followers.

But was this *real person* named Jesus just a charismatic cult liar telling clever tales? "No. We weren't tricked," says Peter,⁸ one of Jesus's first followers. Peter saw with his own eyeballs Jesus do what humans don't do: heal crazy people, cure what doctors couldn't, and raise the dead!⁹

When Jesus physically left Peter, Peter had to choose to continue as a Jesus follower or not. Peter chose Jesus. Peter chose to continue in the Jesus 'way', and what was Peter's reward? Fame? Popularity? Riches?

---

³ 1 Corinthians 15:6 "After that, He appeared to more than five hundred brothers at once, most of whom are still living, though some have fallen asleep."

⁴ Acts 22:4 "I persecuted this Way even to the death, detaining both men and women and throwing them into prison, . . ."

⁵ Romans 8:11 "And if the Spirit of Him who raised Jesus from the dead is living in you, He who raised Christ Jesus from the dead will also give life to your mortal bodies through His Spirit, who lives in you."

⁶ 2 Corinthians 11:24 "Five times I received from the Jews the forty lashes minus one."

⁷ Christians and Muslims alone are more than 50% that have Jesus in their important texts.

⁸ 2 Peter 1:16 "For we did not follow cleverly devised fables when we made known to you the power and coming of our Lord Jesus Christ, but we were eyewitnesses of His majesty."

⁹ Mark 5:1-43.

Not at all. He was arrested[10] and then chose to live in a commune.[11] Would you sign up for that? For a 'charismatic' leader that wasn't even there? Not likely!

Oh, and that guy who approved of killing Jesus's followers,[12] instead gave up his position of power and became a Jesus follower himself, writing about half of our Bible! You may recognize his name — Paul! *Pause and digest — agree, disagree, or discuss?*

Jesus really existed. Jesus was more than a philosopher. Jesus claimed to be God[13] and would make Himself, God, and the Holy Spirit one with each of us.[14]

Jesus is in You. Is that Unsettling?

God is in Jesus. And when you accept the message of Jesus, Jesus is in you. Not, "will be," nor "can be if you do-do-do," *is* in you. Is that profound? Is that unsettling? What are the consequences of that Trinity + You union? *Pause and digest — agree, disagree, or discuss?*

Jesus; Ἰησοῦς; Iésous:
Strong's 2424. "Jesus" is the Greek form of Hebrew Joshua or Yehoshua (YHWH:God + Yasha:saves).
"Christ" is a title meaning "appointed one". Technically He is "Jesus the Christ" which in full translation is "God's appointed one to save us".

If this author came and told you that, "Seeing me is seeing God,"[15] you'd look me over, think I was crazy, and find somewhere else to go. Jesus did just that. Jesus said He was one with God, and then did amazing stuff to prove it.

Who and what *was* Jesus? He was a guy that claimed to be and acted like "God in human form."[16]

Who and what *is* Jesus? Since the rest of what He did and said *was* true, this too *is* true: He joins us to God.

---

[10] Acts 4:3 "They seized Peter and John, and because it was evening, they put them in custody until the next day."

[11] Acts 4:32 "The multitude of believers was one in heart and soul. No one claimed that any of his possessions was his own, but they shared everything they owned."

[12] Acts 22:20 "And when the blood of Your witness Stephen was shed, I stood there giving my approval and watching over the garments of those who killed him."

[13] John 8:24 "That is why I told you that you would die in your sins. For unless you believe that I am He, you will die in your sins."

[14] John 14:20 "On that day you will know that I am in My Father, and you are in Me, and I am in you."

[15] John 14:7 "If you had known Me, you would know My Father as well. From now on you do know Him and have seen Him."

[16] Matthew 1:23 "'Behold, the virgin will be with child and will give birth to a son, and they will call Him Immanuel' (which means, 'God with us')."

Jesus didn't come here to buy us a relationship ticket that is only useful when we die. Jesus doesn't expect us to do good to reach Him. He doesn't expect us to *do* anything but submit to *His way*. Why? Because Jesus is *"the way"*[17] to be one with God, today, *right now*. God in you!

God in Us is Real Transforming Power

And that *is* the miracle of Jesus Christ. Religions make you do-do-do for God. Jesus Christ enables God to be-be-be *in* us, which is *real* transforming power. Hallelujah![18] *Jesus* is the Good News![19]

What is the Key Takeaway?

1. Relationship with Jesus,
    leads to
2. Identity in Jesus,
    leads to
3. Becoming of Jesus.

---

[17] John 14:6 "Jesus answered, "I am the way and the truth and the life. No one comes to the Father except through Me."

[18] Hallelujah, or Hallelu YAH, is a combination of the Hebrew word to 'praise' or 'boast' (H1984 הָלַל halal) and 'Lord' (H3050 יָהּ Yah).

[19] Acts 8:35 "Then Philip began with this very Scripture and told him the good news about Jesus."

5. Spirit, Pneuma 4151

Wind. Breath. Spirit. Ghost. In Greek, the word is "pneuma." In the Bible, pneuma is often joined with the word hagios, "holy", or "of God".[1] Does this Holy Spirit even matter? Should we leave the known physical world for the unknown spiritual world? Should we go to where physical eyes cannot see nor ears hear? God has revealed these answers to us through the exciting experience of the Holy Spirit.[2]

What is the Holy Spirit?

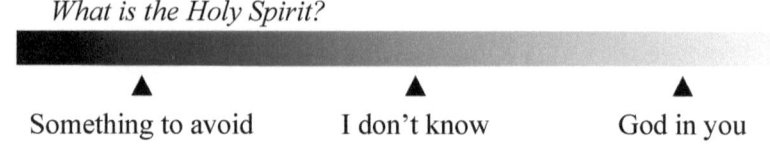

▲	▲	▲
Something to avoid	I don't know	God in you

The Problem

The Bible promises us that once saved, we'll be a new creation,[3] risen with our Savior into a new life.[4] Then why does it feel so often like the old life?

Christians submit to Christ knowing they themselves are not God, that their way isn't working, that they've done not-loving things, and so they _want_ Christ as Lord of their life. Christians _want_ to be better. And then . . . life seems very much the same. We can still think, speak, and do not-loving things, using the same habits of our old self.[5] Who will rescue us from this? Can we change ourselves? *Pause and digest — agree, disagree, or discuss?*

If *you* could change yourself, you would have done it already. You need a power *greater* than yourself to make the changes in you, in the

---

[1] "Spirit" is also the English translation for the Old Testament Hebrew, רוּחַ or "ruach" (H7307), and or "neshamah" (H5397).

[2] 1 Corinthians 2:9-10 "But as it has been written: 'What no eye has seen, and no ear has heard, and has not entered into heart of man, what God has prepared for those loving Him.' For God has revealed it to us through the Spirit. For the Spirit searches all things, even the depths of God.

[3] 2 Corinthians 5:17 "Therefore if anyone is in Christ, he is a new creation. The old has passed away. Behold, the new has come!"

[4] Romans 6:4 "We were therefore buried with Him through baptism into death, in order that, just as Christ was raised from the dead through the glory of the Father, we too may walk in newness of life."

[5] Romans 7:19 "For I do not do the good I want to do. Instead, I keep on doing the evil I do not want to do."

right way, to the right ends. Someone that knows *exactly* what you have been through, how your brain is wired, and loves you. Someone to be *with* you through the process. A potter that can shape *all* the clay that forms you, your past experiences, personality, fears, and abilities, into the *best* new thing.[6]

The Answer

Only God can help you. He can help you *personally,* in your moment of need, now. A book of rules or a god far away in the heavens won't help. God's presence will help. God's peace will help. God with you in life will help.

That is the Holy Spirit. God 'with' you in life, placed inside of you. You are not alone, and never will be alone. God is with you. There is no reason to fear. There is no reason to feel lonely. There is no reason to feel abandoned. The Holy Spirit is ever present within you.

The Holy Spirit is God in You

In John 14:26[7] the Holy Spirit is described as paraklétos (3875), which is translated in English as the comforter, the advocate, or the helper. In Greek paraklétos was the term for a lawyer or advisor that you would call for help, a combination of pará (among or in-the-presence-of, 3844) and kaléō (called, 2564). The Holy Spirit is then the presence of God in you *that we call for help*, advising us in every moment of every hour of your day.

Wait a minute, wait a minute. The Spirit of God is inside of me? Is this author saying something so beautiful can be in someone as dirty as me? YES! And *you* were never 'dirty', only spotted with things not-Holy (defiled, koinoó, 2840), and now you are washed and HOLY! (1 Corinthians 6:11) This author is saying God's Spirit is inside of you because the Bible says so:

> *Do you not know that your body is a temple of the Holy Spirit who is in you, whom you have received from God?*
> *— 1 Corinthians 6:19*

---

[6] Jeremiah 18:4 "But the vessel that he was shaping from the clay became flawed in his hand; so he formed it into another vessel, as it seemed best for him to do."

[7] John 14:26 "But the Advocate, the Holy Spirit, whom the Father will send in My name, will teach you all things and will remind you of everything I have told you."

The Holy Spirit is a gift from God to help us. Are you calling on the power of the Holy Spirit for advice? The Holy Spirit is talking to you.[8] Are you listening?

You need Him. Are you asking?

He's trying to shape your clay. Are you resisting?

Are you submitting and resting in *Him* and *His* timing? Or are you demanding and frustrated at the way *you* want things to go?

Are you afraid He won't complete His work in you? Relax, He will![9] *Pause and digest — agree, disagree, or discuss?*

It's About Union

God doesn't care about the externals. He cares about *you*. He wants a relationship with *you*.[10] He wants a healthy, free-choice relationship that can have open dialogue about your hurts. He wants you to trust that He wants the best for you. He wants you to submit to His love for you.

> **Spirit; πνεῦμα; pneuma:**
> Strong's 4151. Pneuma is the noun form of 'to breathe' or 'blow' (pneó 4154), the life force or soul that God breathed into Adam and all humankind.

Union with the Holy Spirit is that path to have a one-on-one relationship with Jesus Christ, that transforms you into the love that Jesus *is*, from the love that Jesus pours into you. Your change is the result of this all-encompassing Trinity + You relationship. We can't do it ourselves. It is the Holy Spirit that helps us pray.[11] It is the Holy Spirit that sets us free from doing not-loving things.[12] It is the Holy Spirit that teaches us the true way to live in all moments and interactions in our lives.[13]

Our transformation into a loving, holy being flowing with the Holy Spirit can only occur in our calling on the Holy Spirit for help. It is a submission of our will to yearn to do His will, instead of do-do-doing from our own 'good' ideas. We are the branches, and He the root

---

[8] Acts 8:29 "The Spirit said to Philip, 'Go over to that chariot and stay by it.'"

[9] 1 Thessalonians 5:24 "The One who calls you is faithful, and He will do it."

[10] Hosea 6:6 "For I desire mercy, not sacrifice, and [to know (daath H1847)] God rather than burnt offerings."

[11] Romans 8:26 "In the same way, the Spirit helps us in our weakness. For we do not know how we ought to pray, but the Spirit Himself intercedes for us with groans too deep for words."

[12] Romans 8:2 "For in Christ Jesus the law of the Spirit of life set you free from the law of sin and death."

[13] John 16:13 "However, when the Spirit of truth comes, He will guide you into all truth. For He will not speak on His own, but He will speak what He hears, and He will declare to you what is to come."

providing *everything* to sustain life. He is the shepherd, and we the sheep. I pray for this author and all readers to, "have a heart of submission for Him to lead us to His green pastures."[14]

What is the Key Takeaway?

1. Relationship with God's Holy Spirit, leads to
2. Identity in God, which leads to
3. Becoming the love that is God.

---

[14] Psalm 23:2 "He makes me lie down in green pastures; He leads me beside quiet waters."

6. The Do-do Trap

God is Love. Jesus is our bridge. The Holy Spirit is our helper. Now how do we live? Are you a 'good' Christian? Why or why not?

How much time must you dedicate to being a 'good' Christian?

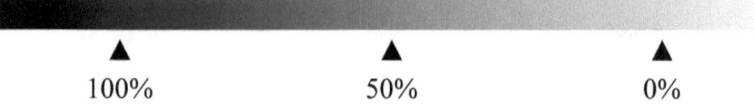

The Problem

Do you complete the Christian 'do-do' list? Do you:
- Go to church when the doors are open?
- Read your Bible?
- Call yourself names with a sneer, like, *"sinner"*?
- Hand out tracts?
- Pray before sunrise?
- Make gospel appointments?
- Attend retreats?
- Guilt others into doing the same?

Or maybe you're a 'good' Christian because you're A+ on the *don't* 'do' list; don't drink, don't dance, don't cuss, and don't dress like 'that'.

Both of these are just <u>*do-do.*</u>

They are both works. You can't get to Heaven with works. Do you think you should live your pre-Heaven life in works? *Pause and digest — agree, disagree, or discuss?*

The Typical Process

It's natural. You become a Christian, and then think, "OK, now what?" So, you immediately begin to fill your life with Christian 'stuff', 'good' things that you think Christians *do.*

We find a church that has some nice music, a not-too long Bible verse sermon, and the service ends with, ". . .and from this lesson, we learn these 5 things that you must *do.*"

Then you read a Christian book, with examples of people doing amazing things, and you think *bad about yourself,* "why can't I be like *that.*" Chapter after chapter they imply to have a great Christian life, even though God didn't craft you as *them*, you have to go do what they *do*.

Somewhere you run across a meme from the year 1896, *'What Would Jesus Do'*.[1] You think, "To be a good Christian, I'll just do what Jesus would do." Except you find out that this doesn't work at all, because you have no idea what Jesus would do to that tailgater that you just brake-checked whose flashing their brights at you now, since (shocker!) you are not Jesus.

You still try to *do* this and *do* that, since you don't know what else *to do*.

All this do-do is the Liar's trap to keep you away from God's relationship with unique you.

Do-do is a Stinking Trap!

Bob George talks about do-do-doing himself into an emotional breakdown for what he thought was 'for God'.[2] He'd hand out tracts, run Bible meetings, make gospel appointments, and preached Jesus to celebrities, until one day on the freeway tears ran down his face from exhaustion. If this was the 'joy in Christ'[3] it was worse than being an atheist!

Praise the Lord that Bob was loved by God into a new direction: *be*ing in Christ. No more do-do in Christ's name, or actions that we cloak with God's light. Bob's life became one where God was tops and his actions *flowed from that*.

The trouble comes when we flip this hierarchy, where instead we put action on top, expecting God and His goodness to *flow from the action*.

---

[1] The full title is, *In His Steps: What Would Jesus Do?* Charles M. Sheldon (ISBN 9781640322493)

[2] *Classic Christianity: Life's Too Short to Miss the Real Thing* Bob George page 15 (ISBN 0890816603)

[3] Philippians 4:4 "Rejoice in the Lord always. I will say it again: Rejoice!"

What works better?
1. God → leads to →Action

or

2. Action → expect it to lead to → God

Pause and digest — agree, disagree, or discuss?

We put action on top all the time. We want to be beautiful, so we buy and do-do a lot of external things and forget about God's beauty.[4] Or we buy and do-do a lot of things to be *happy*.[5] Or do-do things to be *healthy*.[6] Or do-do to be *popular* with people.[7] Or do-do to be a 'good' Christian. Or do-do a zillion other things where we remove God from being on top instead of *starting with God! Pause and digest — agree, disagree, or discuss?*

Put God on Top

Activity is not a relationship. Activity is not submission. Activity doesn't put God first. 'Do this', 'Do that', 'Don't do this', 'Don't do that', are all *works* and not *union* with God. It's the do-do trap![8]

What should the reader *do*? Stop → Drop → Submission

Stop what you are *do*ing, *drop* your knee to the ground or your self-will, and *submit* to God.[9]

- Analyze: Which of your activities are God leading, and which come from other sources? In other words, what is top in your life?

---

[4] 1 Peter 3:4 "... but from the inner disposition of your heart, the unfading beauty of a gentle and quiet spirit, which is precious in God's sight."

[5] Psalm 37:4 "Delight yourself in the LORD, and He will give you the desires of your heart."

[6] Proverbs 17:22 "A joyful heart is good medicine, but a broken spirit dries up the bones."

[7] Galatians 1:10 "Am I now seeking the approval of men, or of God? Or am I striving to please men? If I were still trying to please men, I would not be a servant of Christ."

[8] How many more times can the author insert the phrase, "do-do," without the reader groaning? ... we'll see!

[9] Luke 12:26 "If, then, you cannot even do *the* least, why are you anxious about the rest?"

- Pray: Say something like, "God, help me know your voice.[10] Guide me in your will[11] and not my own." And keep talking and sharing where you are lost and how you need Him. Ask for wisdom in the situation.[12] Then *listen*. Tell God that you are listening. Go about your day and listen, and talk, and listen, and ask, and listen. Yearning your soul towards Him is less *do*, and more *be*. Less structure, and more *relational*.
- Give Up: Do nothing. Rest.[13] Enjoy His creation with thanks in your heart. Laugh, live, love, or buy a different sign from a Christian craft store that pleases you. Or enjoy the taste of a tomato, or the hair curling around your spouse's ear. And say to Him, "Thank you Lord for helping me enjoy the blessings you've placed all over my life. Open my eyes to Your fullness."

People on their death bed regret most their lack of enjoying God's blessings. Why wait to recognize our blessings? Why let darkness steal our light? *Pause and digest — agree, disagree, or discuss?*

Counter Argument

But shouldn't Christian faith produce some *works*?[14] Yes! The reader and author agree! The issue is not the *works*. The issue is the work's *source*.

It isn't 'Christian faith' that produces good works. It is Jesus's goodness that produces good works *through* you. We are not *producers*. We are *conduits*. *Pause and digest — agree, disagree, or discuss?*

People have *good hearts* do-do-doing themselves to exhaustion in very limited types of 'things for God'. God is unlimited! He wants to show love in this world in *unlimited* ways! And He can if we are listening and moving to His guidance. *Pause and digest — agree, disagree, or discuss?*

---

[10] John 10:27 "My sheep listen to My voice; I know them, and they follow Me."

[11] Matthew 6:10 "Your kingdom come, Your will be done, on earth as it is in heaven."

[12] James 1:5 "Now if any of you lacks wisdom, he should ask God, who gives generously to all without finding fault, and it will be given to him."

[13] Hebrews 4:10 "For whoever enters God's rest also rests from his own work, just as God did from His."

[14] James 2:26 "For just as the body apart from spirit is dead, so also faith apart from works is dead."

Let God Lead

God wants a relationship with you. It can't be one-sided, nor have us as the lead. Only in our submission to *His* way and *His* supply can God produce a bounty through us.[15]

Are you getting what this Author is Throwing down?

1. Relationship with God,
    leads to
2. Identity in God,
    leads to
3. God's supply producing His results.

---

[15] 2 Corinthians 9:8 "And God is able to make all grace abound to you, so that in all things, at all times, having all that you need, you will abound in every good work."

7. You, Su 4771

Do you even matter to God? Are we ants; faceless, interchangeable, and disposable? How does your identity in God affect your life?

How does God view you?

▲ Sinner   ▲ Mostly Good   ▲ Saint

High Level

"It's not about you," starts a popular book. But is it really "not about you"? If it's not about you, why did God send Jesus *for you*?[1] If it's not about you, why does God want to be *in* us?[2] Why does God want to use us as His temple, where He resides, His living church in this world?[3]

There is only one logical conclusion.

It *is* about you. And it *is* about God. And it *is* about your relationship *together* in His love.

In a relationship between two free-choice parties, love is a free-choice. Nobody is forced. Nobody is punished. A love-based relationship is free of requirements. Nobody is *used*. The main gain is the *relationship*. If one side doesn't participate, it isn't a relationship. If one side expects the other to do everything, it isn't a relationship. No need to be guilt ridden seeing the truth: The depth of mutual *love* determines the depth of *relationship*.

There are many depths of love and relationships. Human relationships can't all be deep. *How deep can the relationship between you and God be? Pause, and digest — agree, disagree, or discuss?*

---

[1] Luke 15:5 "And when he finds [you], he joyfully puts [you] on his shoulders, . . ."

[2] 1 John 4:13 "By this we know that we remain in Him, and He in us: He has given us of His Spirit."

[3] 1 Peter 2:5 ". . . you also, like living stones, are being built into a spiritual house to be a holy priesthood, offering spiritual sacrifices acceptable to God through Jesus Christ."

A New Identity

When we choose Christ as our Savior, our identity changes. Our old identity gets crucified with Christ. His resurrection produces *our* new identity,[4] eternally alive through Jesus Christ![5]

Choosing Christ as our Savior also means choosing to be a child of God,[6] sharing Christ's glory,[7] with full access to God,[8] and legally adopted by God.[9] Do you *think* of yourself like God thinks of you? Do you *act* like the person that God says you *are*? *Why or why not?*

> **You; σύ; su:**
> Strong's 4771. Can be "you" or "of you" or "your" as in "your God" in Matthew 4:7). Used 2,926 times in all Greek forms.

Your change in identity and relationship is *irrevocable*,[10] just as Christ's resurrection is irrevocable. It doesn't matter if you mess up, God is with you, in you, to help you mature in Him.

What would happen if a sheep suddenly runs away into trouble declaring, "You're not my shepherd!" The sheep still belongs to the shepherd, and that shepherd will bring the sheep back to safety.[11] What the sheep feels or says doesn't change their legal *identity* nor legal *relationship*.

What would happen if a son declared, "You're not my father!" If they say it, does it make it true? The father can always say, "That is my son!"[12] What they feel or say doesn't change their legal identity, nor their legal relationship as inheritors.[13]

---

[4] Romans 6:4 "We were therefore buried with Him through baptism into death, in order that, just as Christ was raised from the dead through the glory of the Father, we too may walk in newness of life."

[5] Romans 6:8 "Now if we died with Christ, we believe that we will also live with Him."

[6] John 1:12 "But to all who did receive Him, to those who believed in His name, He gave the right to become children of God— . . ."

[7] Romans 8:17 "And if we are children, then we are heirs: heirs of God and co-heirs with Christ—if indeed we suffer with Him, so that we may also be glorified with Him."

[8] Ephesians 2:18 "For through Him we both have access to the Father by one Spirit."

[9] Galatians 4:5 ". . . that He might redeem those under the Law, so that we might receive the divine adoption as sons."

[10] Romans 11:29 "For God's gifts and His call are irrevocable."

[11] Luke 15:4 "What man among you, if he has a hundred sheep and loses one of them, does not leave the ninety-nine in the pasture and go after the one that is lost, until he finds it?"

[12] Luke 15:24 "'For this son of mine was dead and is alive again! He was lost and is found!' So they began to celebrate."

[13] 1 Peter 1:4 ". . . and into an inheritance that is imperishable, undefiled, and unfading, reserved in heaven for you, . . ."

God's legal adoption is transformational. The old you of this world is crucified, the new you is born again in His Spirit. What then transforms your life? Your identity as *determined by God.* Should any other opinion matter?

That is why it is *key* for you to *accept* His new identity of you. To think and act as anything less than what *God says we are*, indicates:

1. We think we are right and God wrong.
2. We are thinking and acting as an *identity* that we are not.

Pause and digest — agree, disagree, or discuss?

Do you even matter to God? You have to! Only *unique* you can have the *unique* relationship that you do with God. Are we ants, faceless, interchangeable, and disposable? Of course not! Only unique you can be used by God exactly how you are, where you are, and through who you are. *Pause and digest — agree, disagree, or discuss?*

Your identity in God affects your life. Your relationship with God makes you realize your value to God. He's chosen you (Yes you! Right where you are!) to be His holy representative, showing others how God's loving relationship affects your life,[14] and can affect theirs. No longer do people need to be alone and rejected, they can belong to God by submitting to His love and finally realize how special they are. What should be the impact of that? *Pause and digest — agree, disagree, or discuss?*

Relationship Check

How do you feel when you relate to God? Do you see yourself as a representative of God's family? Is there resistance to what God says you are? Does your flesh refuse to submit to God's word?[15]

Do you feel more comfortable living in the identity of what others call you? Were you brought to Christ with guilt, shame, fear, and doubt messages like:[16]

- Admit you are a sinner.
- God sees you as a lying, thieving, blasphemous adulterer at heart.
- God will punish you in a place called Hell.

---

[14] 1 Peter 2:9 "But you are a chosen people, a royal priesthood, a holy nation, a people for God's own possession, to proclaim the virtues of Him who called you out of darkness into His marvelous light."

[15] Romans 8:7 ". . . because the mind of the flesh is hostile to God: It does not submit to God's law, nor can it do so."

[16] From current and vintage Bible tracts.

- We are lost in sin.
- Someday you will stand before God!
- Are you *sure* you are going to Heaven?

Well, no wonder your identity is filled with guilt, shame, and doubt! Then add the bonus do-do trap guilt of never working enough for man's expectations, and constantly hearing the Liar's mocking, and one sees *why* very little people *want* to share what is *supposed* to be the Good News.

The focus on darkness isn't Good News. Focusing on *Jesus's light* in your life is the Good News! *Pause and digest — agree, disagree, or discuss?*

Jesus's Light is the Good News!

God loves you. God made you unique. He wants you to submit to His plan to have a *relationship with you*, through Jesus Christ. He wants to be *in you*, though His Holy Spirit, to *help you* continue to learn and grow in Love, in *Him*. Like young fruit on the branch, you may not *look* right, you may not be *mature* fruit, but you are *complete* fruit on the vine and complete in Christ.[17]

Guilt, shame, fear and doubt make you a victim, whereas, the love of Christ makes you the *VICTOR*. Which identity have you chosen to fill your life? God says you are the victor and He's in you to prove it.[18] *Pause and digest — agree, disagree, or discuss?*

Guilt, shame, fear and doubt are from the Liar. They are not the fruit of the Spirit. They are not from God. Jesus paid for all the not-loving things you did and will do, why does He need to die again and again and again for you to be free? Jesus knows what you did, what happened to you, and your entire future, and He paid it all. Why then are you chained back from a fuller relationship with God?

It is OK to feel guilt, shame, and fear for things in the past, as this remorse guides us from doing it again, but not to live there. The past and those feelings should not separate you from the love of God when Jesus has done all to reunite you into a relationship with the Trinity.

Ask for God to help you *know you are free*, regardless of how you feel, since in truth, you already *are* free! If memories or the Liar remind you of who you *were*, take a stand against them and say, "Jesus already

---

[17] Colossians 2:10 "And you have been made complete in Christ, who is the head over every ruler and authority."

[18] 1 Corinthians 15:57 "But thanks be to God, who gives us the victory through our Lord Jesus Christ!"

knows about that, took care of it, and He loves me for who I was and who I am. That was the old me, but not the new me. And when I mess up again, Jesus knew about that too and took care of it too!" *Pause and digest — agree, disagree, or discuss?*

God Sees Us Clean, and Our Conscience Should Be Too[19]

What does God say about you?
    He says I'm perfectly loved by Him.[20]
From when?
    Forever.[21]
How long does it last?
    Forever.[22]
And when you accepted Jesus, what did that make *you*?
    Complete.[23]
How much does He know about you?
    Everything.[24]
Everything?
    Everything.
Knowing everything, how did God *choose* to make *you*?
    Special.[25]
Being special and complete forever, when is God with you?
    Always.[26]
What then is holding you back from God's love?
    Acceptance.

---

[19] 2 Corinthians 5:11 "What we are is clear to God, and I hope it is clear to your conscience as well."

[20] Psalm 18:30 "As for God, His way is perfect; the word of the LORD is flawless. He is a shield to all who take refuge in Him."

[21] Ephesians 1:4 "For He chose us in Him before the foundation of the world to be holy and blameless in His presence. In love . . ."

[22] 1 Chronicles 16:34 "Give thanks to the LORD, for He is good; His loving devotion endures forever."

[23] Hebrews 10:14 "For by one offering, He has [completed, finished, perfected, (teleioó, 5048)] for all time those being made holy."

[24] Psalm 139:1 "O LORD, You have searched me and known me."

[25] Psalm 139:14 "I praise You, for I am fearfully and [distinct, separated, set apart, wonderful (palah H6395)] made. Marvelous are Your works, and I know this very well."

[26] Deuteronomy 31:8 "The LORD Himself goes before you; He will be with you. He will never leave you nor forsake you. Do not be afraid or discouraged."

God has done His part, and wants to do more in your life. Will you let Him?

What's the Summary?

God is *Love*,
Accept His love, so that
You can love others
As you and they are able
As He loves you.

8. Submission, Hupotassó 5293

Is submission painful? Is it weak? Is it evil?[1] How does one submit to God? Must one submit and if so, how often?

What does 'submission to God' mean to you?

▲	▲	▲
Fear any action without God's specific biblical consent.	Do your own thing. Find a verse to affirm your stance.	Dance with one Spirit.

One Way to Know

If you read all the cookbooks in the world, but never cook, and never eat, you can talk and debate endlessly *about* cooking, but what will you actually *know* of cooking, or taste, or harmony of ingredients?

Likewise, though you read the Bible every day, and go to church, but never submit to the voice of the Spirit, what will you actually *know* of Love, or people relationships?

The typical Christian process creates *law-scholars*, when God wants *servants*.[2] The law-scholar talks and debates *about* God, wraps their righteousness in big words, but chokes off God's living water that powers *His* work.[3] *Pause and digest — agree, disagree, or discuss?*

Jesus had some tough words about law-scholars that promote those do-do works without submitting to God's Spirit in Luke 11:52:

> *Woe to you experts in the law! For you have taken away the key to knowledge. You yourselves have not entered, and you have hindered those who were entering.*

---

[1] Romans 8:1 "Therefore *there is* now no condemnation to those in Christ Jesus."

[2] Mark 10:43 "But it shall not be this way among you. Instead, whoever wants to become great among you must be your servant, ..."

[3] 1 Timothy 1:4 "... or devote themselves to myths and endless genealogies, which promote speculation rather than the stewardship of God's work, which is by faith."

What is the "key to knowledge" that enables us to be transformed?[4] The Holy Spirit.[5]

Just after Jesus's ascension, there were no 'letters', and therefore no Bible! The disciples *had to rely* on the Holy Spirit[6] for their knowledge and transformation. Even when there were parts of the Bible starting to circulate (estimated around 50 AD), Peter admits Paul's letters are "hard to understand"![7] Submitting[8] to the Holy Spirit was the best way to know what was *true* living water, and what was *distortion*. Let us do the same.

How do we get guidance from the Holy Spirit? As a branch, we must not choke off the living water that comes only from the vine. God has wisdom *specific to you* and *your current situation* that won't come from this book, or the internet — it comes from God through Christ to the Holy Spirit in you. This is the Trinity + You relationship. General principles can come from the Bible, but the Holy Spirit sees all things from all sides to know how to act, or not, specific to *this moment* in *your life*.

Let the Living Water Flow!

How does this play out applying the Bible and the Holy Spirit? The Bible's general principle of Proverbs 26:4-5 says to <u>both</u> answer a fool and don't answer a fool. The Holy Spirit gives discretion <u>which</u> to do in *this specific moment* in *your life.*[9] *Pause and digest — agree, disagree, or discuss?*

What is God's 'light' that shines through us? What is His 'living water' that flows through us? Love! God is Love! His love, *Himself*, is this 'fluid' that comes from God, is God's Holy Spirit, that flows to us and through us, so that we can 'love' others (or flow God's Holy Spirit to others) — if we accept His love of us!

---

[4] Philippians 3:21 ". . . who, by the power that enables Him to subject all things to Himself, will transform our lowly bodies to be like His glorious body."

[5] 1 John 2:27 "And as for you, the anointing you received from Him remains in you, and you do not need anyone to teach you. But just as His true and genuine anointing teaches you about all things, so remain in Him as you have been taught."

[6] Acts 16:7 "And when they came to the border of Mysia, they tried to enter Bithynia, but the Spirit of Jesus would not permit them."

[7] 2 Peter 3:16 "Some parts of his letters are hard to understand, which ignorant and unstable people distort, as they do the rest of the Scriptures, to their own destruction."

[8] 1 Corinthians 14:32 "The spirits of prophets are subject to prophets."

[9] Proverbs 26:4-5 "Do not answer a fool according to his folly, or you yourself will be like him. Answer a fool according to his folly, lest he become wise in his own eyes."

Only submitting yourself to God's love,[10] letting God's love flow through you as the branch, asking and listening to the Holy Spirit, do you produce the fruit of the vine; love that is full, juicy fruit.

Are you producing only dry fruit without the living water in it? Talk to God about that. Ask and listen to Him, and listen and listen. God wants you to rely on Him, which *is* submission, letting go, and dropping the burden of trying to do it yourself. Submission to God isn't weak or painful. To let Him Love you through this Trinity + You relationship you realize how much strength you have in love. Love in power. Love without fear[11] since you are spiritually invincible in God's love expressed through unique you.

Not 'self-produced-love', it is submitting to God-produced-love.[12] Not 'you be Jesus'. It is Jesus *in you* flowing *through you* as living water from the vine, to the branch, to the fruit. *Pause and digest — agree, disagree, or discuss?*

The Fruit of the Spirit (Galatians 5:22-23) are all *spiritual things:* love, joy, peace, patience, kindness, goodness, faithfulness, gentleness, self-control. These are not physical things and can't be physically measured with a ruler or scale.

To fully live in the joy of the Trinity, we are at a point in our relationship maturity where *physical* understanding stops. Where the *physical* do-do rules and do-do formulas stop. Where the *physical* law-scholars can help no further.

To experience and express God's love, to fully live,[13] *you must have a spiritual relationship with the Holy Trinity*. Not a physical one, since He isn't physically sitting next to you. A *spiritual* relationship. A spiritual relationship with Jesus Christ on top, as your leader, with you trusting Him to know, guide, and strengthen *you* how to be your best and live your best in every moment.[14]

We must ask Jesus to help us submit to living through *His* love in our heart. This is a submission from desire, not forced upon us. We want

---

[10] 1 Corinthians 15:28 "And when all things have been subjected to Him, then the Son Himself will be made subject to Him who put all things under Him, so that God may be all in all."

[11] 2 Timothy 1:7 "For God has not given us a spirit of fear, but of power, love, and self-control."

[12] Romans 10:3 "Because they were ignorant of God's righteousness and sought to establish their own, they did not submit to God's righteousness."

[13] Hebrews 12:9 "Should we not much more submit to the Father of our spirits and live?"

[14] John 4:24 "God is Spirit, and His worshipers must worship Him in spirit and in truth."

to see and hear as the Holy Spirit does *spiritually* in every moment of our spiritual *and* physical existence.

The physical world is often a reflection of the spiritual. We want to love as Jesus did,[15] which we can only do if we let Him as love flow through us. *Love* is spiritual. It can't be measured with a physical scale. The Trinity + You relationship is our path to let *Him* love through *us*. We then can *exist as physical* beings while *interacting as the spiritual beings* that we are and will *continue to be* in Heaven.

The physical you is temporary. The spiritual you is eternal. Here is a joke about that. Why does the flesh battle the spirit?[16] Because it's not going with you!

There is No Formula for a Trinity + You Relationship

There are no written rules, no formula, for this submission to the Trinity by unique-you interacting with unique-others, which is why law-scholars have to stop before here — there is nothing to blab about and no books to sell. You simply need to ask, "God, what should I be doing here?"

It feels *unnatural* to live in the spirit, as our life-experiences are all as fleshly physical beings. But it is the spiritual realm that Jesus was tied to and wants us to live, in one union, knowing God.[17] He wants us to leave the formulas and written rules (the law of stone) and live in the Holy Spirit (the law of love)[18] as detailed in Romans 6 through 8, because:

1. Love fulfills the Old Testament laws of stone.[19]
2. The Holy Spirit's love is perfect in every situation.
3. Any 'formula' or 'rule' *limits God's love!*

Pause and digest — agree, disagree, or discuss?

---

[15] 1 John 4:7 "Beloved, let us love one another, because love comes from God. Everyone who loves has been born of God and knows God."

[16] Galatians 5:17 "For the flesh craves what is contrary to the Spirit, and the Spirit what is contrary to the flesh. They are opposed to each other, so that you do not do what you want."

[17] Ephesians 3:16 "I ask that out of the riches of His glory He may strengthen you with power through His Spirit in your inner being, . . ."

[18] John 15:10 "If you keep My commandments, you will remain in My love, just as I have kept My Father's commandments and remain in His love."

[19] Romans 13:10 "Love does no wrong to its neighbor. Therefore love is the fulfillment of the law."

Listen

Still, how *does* one tune-in to the Holy Spirit? Speak to the Holy Spirit as only you can. Listen and speak. Listen. Listen and speak and listen. This is a relationship in love.

When you encounter the physical, do the same, interacting as the spiritual being that you are. If a person looks disturbed, ask God, "What should I do with this person right now?" And listen to Him!

When you go on vacation, choose what to wear, or pick a sermon to listen to online, ask God about it. This may sound ridiculous, or you may resist the idea,[20] but soon you won't need to ask with your physical words as you will ask with *your spirit*. You will *know* His gentle guidance as the shepherd and submit as the trusting sheep.[21] Your 'desires' will be in-tune and in union with His 'desires'.

Note also that the Shepherd is not directing every movement. We're not robots, so you *don't* need to ask God for everything or be paralyzed from being out of 'God's will'. You are *always* God's sheep. Your desire to do God's will *is* His will so you are *always in* 'God's will'. The intent is that you are always thinking and moving and dancing to God's guidance, and no other.

You may waver away from God's voice, or be distracted by noise of this world,[22] but it is our job to keep tuning in to God's perfect note, the law of Love.

> **Submission; ὑποτάσσω; hupotassó:**
> Strong's 5293. A combination of the words 'arranged' 'under', indicating a clear and understood hierarchy. Usually a choice.

Caution! The Liar pretends to be God's voice.[23] Test these messages that you hear and only keep what produces the good fruit of Love.[24] The Bible is a great foundation for this testing, one that Jesus used Himself.[25] As your relationship strengthens, the Liar, the

---

[20] Romans 8:7 "... because the mind of the flesh is hostile to God: It does not submit to God's law, nor can it do so."

[21] John 10:4 "When he has brought out all his own, he goes on ahead of them, and his sheep follow him because they know his voice."

[22] Luke 10:40 "But Martha was distracted by all the preparations to be made. She came to Jesus and said, 'Lord, do You not care that my sister has left me to serve alone? Tell her to help me!'"

[23] 2 Corinthians 11:14 "And no wonder, for Satan himself masquerades as an angel of light."

[24] 1 Thessalonians 5:21 "... but test all things. Hold fast to what is good."

[25] Matthew 4:4 "But Jesus answered, 'It is written: "Man shall not live on bread alone, but on every word that comes from the mouth of God."'"

counterfeit, will also become more easily recognized.[26] Ignore these demons as you have power over them in Christ.[27]

Love God. Listen. Submit. He is talking just to you, for you are unique and special to Him. You are a Victor with Christ![28]

What is the Key Takeaway?

God is Love,
Submit to His love, so that
You can love others.

---

[26] Romans 8:2 "For in Christ Jesus the law of the Spirit of life set you free from the law of sin and death."

[27] Luke 10:17 "The seventy-two returned with joy and said, 'Lord, even the demons submit to us in Your name.'"

[28] 1 Corinthians 15:57 "But thanks be to God, who gives us the victory through our Lord Jesus Christ!"

9. Trinity + You Bread

Everyone gets a break. Why not authors and readers? We've been hitting this thing pretty hard now and, if you are like the author, you probably could use a snack. And maybe you are also wondering how the Trinity + You (God, Jesus, Holy Spirit, + You) can be both 'separate, distinct, and unique' while also being 'one'.[1] This Trinity + You bread recipe will demonstrate.

	volume	*oz*	*gram*	*shekel*[2]
Flour	3 cups	13	360	32
Milk	1 cup	8	240	21
Salt	1 tsp	0.35	10	1
Yeast	2 tsp / 1 packet	0.2	6	0.5

Mix all ingredients together at 77°F / 25°C until thoroughly blended. Adjust the liquid and flour as necessary so that all the flour is moistened and comes together into a single lump.

| Add Ingredients | Thoroughly Blend | After Second Knead |

If you want to express your uniqueness or are moved by the Spirit, add a few spoons of fat and or sugar and or anything else you think might be tasty.

Cover to prevent drying out (either with oil, a moist towel, or a big pan), and let rest for 10 minutes. Uncover the dough, wet your hands, grab one side of the dough and stretch it straight up as far as it will go without breaking, then let it fall on itself. Keep doing this until it forms

---

[1] John 17:21 ". . . that all of them may be one, as You, Father, are in Me, and I am in You. May they also be in Us, so that the world may believe that You sent Me."

[2] Here, a shekel is 11.4g (0.0114kg). A talent (34.2kg) is 60 minas, a mina (0.57kg) is 50 shekels. Shekel in the Bible was both weight (and eventually coinage) whose weight varied through time, so your own recipe in shekels may vary.

a rough ball (or knead it as you like). If the dough ball has big lumpy bits in it, repeat the dough stretching again in 10 minutes.[3]

Cover the dough and wait for the dough to double in size (about 90 minutes). Make yourself a nice cup of tea and count your blessings.

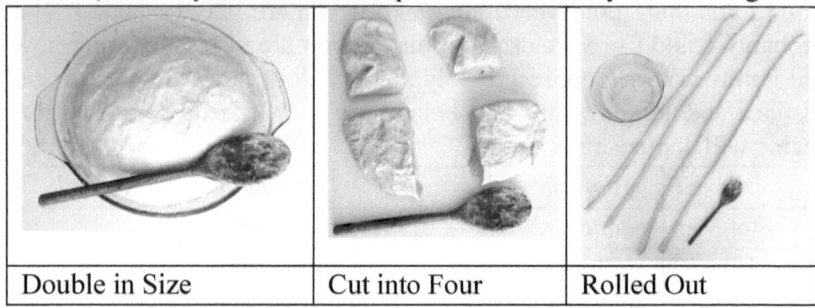

| Double in Size | Cut into Four | Rolled Out |

After the dough doubles, cut it into four pieces. Roll, squish, or pull each piece into a cylinder of about 3 feet / 1 meter. Take the ends of all four pieces and pinch them together to make them a single point. If you have the skill, *braid* these four pieces *loosely* together and pinch the final ends. If you are endowed like Elisha,[4] or don't have the skill, *twist* these pieces *loosely* together and pinch the final ends.

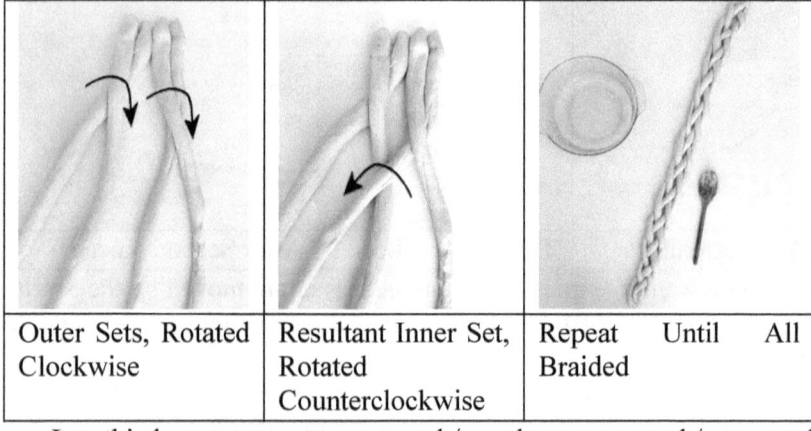

| Outer Sets, Rotated Clockwise | Resultant Inner Set, Rotated Counterclockwise | Repeat Until All Braided |

Lay this long rope on to a greased / parchment covered / cornmeal dusted pan in the shape of a heart, circle, or anything you want.

If you want the crust to glisten, brush now with milk, fat, egg, or sugar. Cover, and let double in size, about 60 minutes.

---

[3] This author had to add 25% more milk and knead it two times.

[4] 2 Kings 2:23 "From there, Elisha went up to Bethel, and as he was walking up the road, a group of boys came out of the city and jeered at him, chanting, 'Go up, you baldhead! Go up, you baldhead!'"

Bake until golden brown at 375°F / 190°C / Gas Mark 5, which should be 30-40 minutes.

This Bread is Unique

But what just happened? This recipe is so basic it requires you to add *yourself* to it. You are different than every other reader. Which milk and flour did you buy and add? Did you add butter, corn oil, bacon grease, something else or nothing extra? Did you mix the dough a bit more or less? Do you like to keep your kitchen temperatures a bit colder or warmer changing the time to double in size? Therefore, this bread is unique, just like you, and just like the Trinity + You is unique.

The Trinity + You is Unique

Slice off a piece to eat while you think about these things. Even your slice size and topping choice are unique!

Do you see four distinct pieces on the outside of the bread? Yes? What about the inside? No? The *outside* is 'separate, distinct, and unique' while the inside is 'one', just like Trinity + You are designed to be *one*.

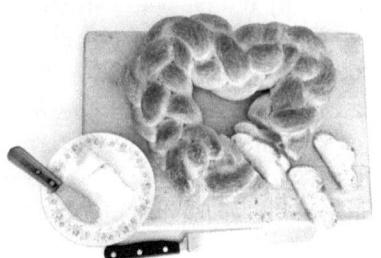

Have another slice as you think about these things.

God tells us to love Him and love others. The only way to fully understand love, is to *be* love, to *be one with Him*.

Be One with the Bread of Life

Let us be one with the Bread of Life,[5] to do the will of God[6] merged uniquely with God, Jesus, the Holy Spirt, and you, as the Trinity + You.

---

[5] John 6:35 "Jesus answered, 'I am the bread of life. Whoever comes to Me will never hunger, and whoever believes in Me will never thirst.'"

[6] John 6:38 "For I have come down from heaven, not to do My own will, but to do the will of Him who sent Me."

10. Heart, Kardia 2588

You have it. God wants it.[1] It holds your treasure.[2] It produces your actions.[3] It lets you <u>see</u> God.[4] It gets you into Heaven.[5] Did you guess what 'it' is? It's your heart.

What does 'heart' mean in the Bible?

▲ Rules of Stone   ▲ Thoughts   ▲ Desires

High Level

Submitting to Christ should produce positive changes in your life. If not, why bother with Christianity? Christianity *does* produce positive changes if we *use* the gift given to us. The gift given to us when we become a Christian is a new heart.[6] The heart is Christ's.[7]

'Heart' is a *yearning desire* for God and His ways to shape your life. Your heart's desires determine if you pridefully try to *be* God, or submit to live *in* God. Good or evil, the start is the heart.[8] *Pause and digest — agree, disagree, or discuss?*

Yearn for God

Are God's desires for us the same in the Old and New Testament? Yes, since God is unchanging. Who did God select to be king and

---

[1] Mark 12:30 "Love the Lord your God with all your heart and with all your soul and with all your mind and with all your strength."

[2] Matthew 6:21 "For where your treasure is, there your heart will be also."

[3] Proverbs 4:23 "Guard your heart with all diligence, for from it flow springs of life."

[4] Matthew 5:8 "Blessed are the pure in heart, for they will see God."

[5] Romans 10:9 ". . . that if you confess with your mouth, 'Jesus is Lord,' and believe in your heart that God raised Him from the dead, you will be saved."

[6] Ezekiel 36:26 "I will give you a new heart and put a new spirit within you; I will remove your heart of stone and give you a heart of flesh."

[7] 2 Corinthians 3:3 "It is clear that you are a letter from Christ, the result of our ministry, written not with ink but with the Spirit of the living God, not on tablets of stone but on tablets of human hearts."

[8] Luke 6:45 "The good man brings good things out of the good treasure of his heart, and the evil man brings evil things out of the evil treasure of his heart. For out of the overflow of the heart, the mouth speaks."

patriarch to Christ? God selected David. David did some messed up some things, but what did David do right? He *yearned* for God, "As the deer yearns for water, so my soul yearns after You, O God." (Psalm 42:1) Let us also yearn for God, always.

Yearning for God is a stance of submission. Submitting to God lets the Spirit make positive changes in us.[9] By submitting, we draw guidance and energy from Christ by us being 'in Christ'.[10] The result? We spread His sweetness by being *in* His sweetness.[11]

> **Heart; καρδία; kardia:** Strong's 2588. Usage: the heart; mind, character, inner self, will, intention, center. Our moral preference, desire-producers that from the fruit produced clearly show who we really *are*.

The opposite of submission is where *we* try to 'be good'. When *we* draw guidance and energy *from ourselves,* it is based on our own rules and ideas that aren't 100% from love and mercy.[12] Paul calls this a "stone" heart resulting in a "ministry of death".[13] We slide into becoming hard-hearted, prideful, and selfish — *a modern-day Pharisee.*

The sign of being a modern-day Pharisee is when you fall into the do-do trap of rules and activities which become a *more important goal than* being filled with and outflowing God's love and mercy —

- ✓ Do-do this: church attendance, tithe, daily Bible, daily prayer, pray before you eat, conferences.
- ✓ Don't do this: swear,[14] smoke, drink, laugh, smile, cry, get mad, fight back, dance.

Following these do-do 'rules', by themselves, *can* produce good fruit, but they are like dancing without hearing the music, which can lead to waltzing to disco music! Or in the spiritual realm, dancing

---

[9] 2 Corinthians 3:6 "And He has qualified us as ministers of a new covenant, not of the letter but of the Spirit; for the letter kills, but the Spirit gives life."

[10] 2 Corinthians 2:17 "On the contrary, in Christ we speak before God with sincerity, as men sent from God."

[11] 2 Corinthians 2:14 "But thanks be to God, who always leads us triumphantly as captives in Christ and through us spreads everywhere the fragrance of the knowledge of Him."

[12] Matthew 9:13 "But go and learn what this means: 'I desire mercy, not sacrifice.' For I have not come to call the righteous, but sinners."

[13] 2 Corinthians 3:7-8 "Now if the ministry of death, which was engraved in letters on stone, came with such glory that the Israelites could not gaze at the face of Moses because of its fleeting glory, will not the ministry of the Spirit be even more glorious?"

[14] Matthew 26:74 "Then he began to curse and to swear, 'I do not know the man!' And immediately a rooster crowed."

without the music made by the music-maker, Jesus, can also lead to some not-love missteps!

Do-do-doing or don't-do-doing doesn't help *your love* be the love *of God's*. It helps your love *act like, seem like, and sound like* the love of God's but never *be* the love of God's. Do you see the danger of this? *Pause and digest — agree, disagree, or discuss?*

God's love is unlimited![15] Only *through Him* can our love be unlimited too by getting it *from Him*. Love is more important than rules and specific activities. Do-do or don't-do doesn't matter. What matters is your relationship to Jesus Christ since knowing He loves you will automatically make you want to be right from your gratitude and thankfulness of His loving you (and not from the guilt or obligation of trying to keep His love since He already loves you!).[16] Yearn for Him and *He* will guide you. Knowing and doing 'the right thing' can only flow from Jesus Christ.

There are too many people do-do-doing 'Christianity' that won't bow their hearts to Christ.[17] Are we different than Adam and Eve trying to be our own God? *Pause and digest — agree, disagree, or discuss?*

If our hearts yearn for God, the Holy Spirit can write a whole new definition of 'you'. No longer are 'you' what your parents called you. No longer are 'you' what people label you. No longer can the world define 'you' by putting their voices in your head.

God knows what you were, what you are, what He is working you to be, and He is lovingly devoted to you.[18] Believe *Him*.

Believe God

It is God's opinion that matters now. Those ads designed to make you feel bad about yourself — they are powerless clamor. Those memories of rejection repeating in your head — they don't have any strength. That's the old 'you'. God made the new 'you' in Him,[19] and those messages don't apply to Him + You.

You can say with all truth of God:

---

[15] Ephesians 3:18 You "will have power, together with all the saints, to comprehend the length and width and height and depth" of the Love of Christ.

[16] John 15:9 "As the Father has loved Me, I also have loved you. Abide in My Love."

[17] Matthew 15:8 "These people honor Me with their lips, but their hearts are far from Me."

[18] Psalm 31:7 "I will be glad and rejoice in Your loving devotion, for You have seen my affliction; You have known the anguish of my soul."

[19] Colossians 3:10 ". . . and have put on the new self, which is being renewed in knowledge in the image of its Creator."

"That's not me anymore. I was those things and did those things, and I wish I didn't, but that's not *me* now. I may hear those old voices, but that is not *me*. Those things don't control *me* anymore. I am free. I am free because God loves *me*. He's making an even better *me*, the person that He created *me* to be!" *Pause and digest — agree, disagree, or discuss?*

That's NOT Me

Joining God, Jesus, and the Holy Spirit in a Trinity + You relationship enables your positive change. Our heart as God's heart is how God wants us to use our new heart. How does this work in day-to-day life?

In Heaven, when we sing[20] where does the sound come from? Will we only be *spiritual* bodies[21] with no hunger or thirst?[22] Will there be air to physically vibrate our vocal cords? Only God knows. This author speculates the singing will come from the *spiritual* sound we make, "groaning inwardly" from the desires of our hearts (kardia, inner self).[23]

Here on earth we can also sing to the Lord through our heart. It is fine to sing with our mouths, but without the heart yearning for God, the song is noise.[24] Yearn for God. Sing from your heart yearning for Him. Even without sound, *God can hear your heart's song.*[25]

Your heart can be heard by God. Your heart can also *hear* God![26] How does one *hear* love? In your heart. God's music are the songs of love, mercy, and compassion. How do you hear them? As best we can on earth, as in Heaven, without physical ears, our *hearts* must listen for God's music.

---

[20] Revelation 5:12 "In a loud voice they were saying: 'Worthy is the Lamb who was slain, to receive power and riches and wisdom and strength and honor and glory and blessing!'"

[21] 1 Corinthians 15:44 "It is sown a natural body; it is raised a spiritual body. If there is a natural body, there is also a spiritual body."

[22] Revelation 7:16 "Never again will they hunger, and never will they thirst; nor will the sun beat down upon them, nor any scorching heat."

[23] Romans 8:23 "Not only that, but we ourselves, who have the firstfruits of the Spirit, groan inwardly as we wait eagerly for our adoption as sons, the redemption of our bodies."

[24] Psalm 66:18 "If I had cherished iniquity in my heart, the Lord would not have listened."

[25] Romans 8:27 "And He who searches our hearts knows the mind of the Spirit, because the Spirit intercedes for the saints according to the will of God."

[26] 1 Kings 3:9 "Therefore give Your servant a [hearing (shama H8085)] heart to judge Your people and to discern between good and evil. For who is able to govern this great people of Yours?"

And if you *listen* to God's music, you will begin to *sing* His songs. If you hear His love, you will begin to *be* His love. Your heart will beat with His heart. His peace will be your peace.[27]

Open Your Heart[28]

Union with the Trinity, as the Trinity + You, starts your positive changes. Union occurs when your heart submits to God's heart. Submit your heart to God and be changed into glory.[29]

What's the Heart of the Matter?

1. Union with the Trinity,
    leads to
2. Your heart's identity in the Trinity,
    leads to
3. Becoming of the Trinity.

---

[27] John 14:27 "Peace I leave with you; My peace I give to you. I do not give to you as the world gives. Do not let your hearts be troubled; do not be afraid."

[28] Ephesians 1:18 "I ask that the eyes of your heart may be enlightened, . . ."

[29] 2 Corinthians 3:18 "And we, who with unveiled faces all reflect the glory of the Lord, are being transformed into His image with intensifying glory, which comes from the Lord, who is the Spirit."

11. Just in Case

Just in case you are not a Christian, and want to be one right now so that Jesus is Lord of your life, simply speak in agreement this statement below and live as such going forward, yearning always for God.

Lord Jesus, please come into my heart and fill me with your Holy Spirit[1] as I want you to be Lord of my life, now and forever. I believe[2] that you died for my sins so I didn't have to. I believe you were resurrected[3] giving me eternal life so I could be with you forever. Thank you for such a beautiful gift.

Thank you for loving me Jesus. Even though it's hard to accept your love, it is my heart's desire to know how much you love me[4] so that I can also love others with your same love.[5] In your name I pray, Lord Jesus Christ, Amen.

---

[1] Acts 13:52 "And the disciples were filled with joy and with the Holy Spirit."

[2] Acts 16:31 "They replied, 'Believe in the Lord Jesus and you will be saved, you and your household.'"

[3] Romans 10:9 ". . . that if you confess (homologeó, 3670, speak in agreement) with your mouth, 'Jesus is Lord,' and <u>believe in your heart</u> that God raised Him from the dead, you will be saved."

[4] Ephesians 3:16-19 "I ask that out of the riches of His glory He may strengthen you with power through <u>His Spirit in your inner being</u>, so that <u>Christ may dwell in your hearts</u> through faith. Then you, being rooted and grounded in love, will have power, together with all the saints, to comprehend the length and width and height and depth of <u>the love of Christ, and to know this love</u> that surpasses knowledge, that you may be filled with all the fullness of God.

[5] 1 John 4:12 "No one has ever seen God; but if we love one another, God abides in us, and His love is perfected in us."

12. New, Kainos 2537

How can we be 'new' bowing our hearts to Christ? How does this work? What does this look like? What does the 'new' mean?

What does 'new' mean to God?

▲   ▲

Different Actions   Different Power

Questions

What is the source for:
1. *Decision* to change your life?
2. *Ability* to change your life?
3. *Reduced* desire to return to the 'old' way?

When we bow our heart to Christ, we are open to the Holy Spirit's guidance. Instead of poorly imitating what is 'good', God *makes* us 'good.'[1] The old life-drivers are gone and replaced with God's life-drivers of love.[2]

Here are the details of the new Trinity + You relationship:

Old: Separated God	New: With God
Separated from God. Isaiah 59:2 — "But your iniquities have built barriers between you and your God, and your sins have hidden His face from you, so that He does not hear."	Always with God. Isaiah 59:20-21 — "'The Redeemer will come to Zion, to those in Jacob who turn from transgression,' declares the LORD. 'As for Me, this is My covenant with them,' says the LORD. 'My Spirit will not depart from you, and My words that I have put in your mouth will not depart from your mouth or from the mouths of your children and grandchildren, from now on and forevermore,' says the LORD."

---

[1] Ephesians 2:10 "For we are God's workmanship, created in Christ Jesus to do good works, which God prepared in advance as our way of life."

[2] Hebrews 8:13 "By speaking of a new covenant, He has made the first one obsolete; and what is obsolete and aging will soon disappear."

The Do-Do Trap 57

When our ways are not God's ways, with the wrong heart we ask for the wrong things so God doesn't respond to unholy asks ("Let these be the winning lottery numbers God!"). Those that bow their heart to the Redeemer (Jesus) get a new heart in union with God,[3] so that our asks *change* to align with His will and His goodness ("God help me love others, cause I'm not feeling like it today!").[4]

Now even when we mess up, we're *never* separated. <u>*God with us is the Way*</u>, always.[5]

Case	Old Way: Separated God	New Way: With God, Always
When we do 'not-loving' things:	God | You	God + You

Living in union as the Trinity + You, our *source* of change, changes:

Case	Old Way: Separated God	New Way: With God
Your source to change:	Change from fear of punishment or rejection.	Change from healing (no longer be 'broken') and comforting love (no longer feel 'empty').

As the Trinity + You, our *ability* to change, changes:

Case	Old Way: Separated God	New Way: With God
Your ability to change:	-No tools or help but our own. -Will run out of power and energy.	-Union with God is our help. -God's power is unlimited.

---

[3] Ephesians 3:17 "... so that Christ may dwell in your hearts through faith."

[4] 1 John 5:14 "And this is the confidence that we have before Him: If we ask anything according to His will, He hears us."

[5] Emmanuël DeWeg, altijd (if you want to say the whole thing in Dutch).

As the Trinity + You, our *motivation* changes the results:

Case	Old Way: Separated God	New Way: With God
Your results:	-Never good 'enough' -Process pushes us away from relationships (God and others). -We give up, sin more, spiral worse.	-*No fear* of rejection or punishment. -*Peace* as you are and yearning for more purity. -*Yearn* for fuller relationships. -Mess up but get up, and keep heading into God's love.

Which love is healthier? Beatings or hugs? Which produces longer lasting and better change? In the *now*, you may fail, but you are never a fail-<u>ure</u> (an identity).

A New Identity

Your identity changed when you bowed your heart to Christ. Your *relationship* to God and others changed. This gets to the center of the issue. How you <u>see yourself</u> will produce your actions and responses. *Pause and digest — agree, disagree, or discuss?*

Your actions and responses changed because of God's proclamation of *who* you are (glorified,[6] a saint,[7] an inheritor[8], a son or daughter of God[9]).

Your actions and responses changed because *you are* His temple, with the Holy Spirit inside of you at all times in life.[10]

God is showing you that He loves *you!* Because of all these things, of course your actions and responses are more likely to start with Jesus.[11] *Pause and digest — agree, disagree, or discuss?*

---

[6] Romans 8:30 "And those He predestined, He also called; those He called, He also justified; those He justified, He also glorified."

[7] Romans 1:7 "To all those being in Rome beloved of God, called saints."

[8] Ephesians 1:18-19 ". . . that you may know the hope of His calling, the riches of His glorious inheritance in the saints, and the surpassing greatness of His power to us who believe."

[9] Galatians 3:26 "You are all sons of God through faith in Christ Jesus."

[10] 1 Corinthians 3:16 "Do you not know that you yourselves are God's temple, and that God's Spirit dwells in you?"

[11] 1 Corinthians 6:20 ". . . you were bought at a price. Therefore glorify God with

As the Trinity + You, we can see the difference in the *actions* of our life:

Case	Old Way: Separated God	New Way: With God
Actions:	"I got to get clean *first,* then go to Jesus." (No one ever got 'clean' and then found Jesus)	"I need *Jesus* first, then can get clean." (People say, "I found Jesus and then got clean."

As the Trinity + You, we see the difference in our *feelings*:

Case	Old Way: Separated God	New Way: With God
Feelings:	"I'm not worth it. God doesn't love me. I'm getting what I deserve — emptiness, abuse by self and others, lack of love, and full of empty consumption of anything to feel good."	"I may not be worthy, but I'm worth it.[12] God tells me so. He sent Jesus to prove it. I put stuff out of my life (abuse, empty consumption, bad responses) since that *is not me* in Jesus.

As the Trinity + You, we see the difference in our *thoughts*:

Case	Old Way: Separated God	New Way: With God
Thoughts:	"God is away from me. I might as well continue doing anything to feel good. I'm already separated from God, what do I have to lose?"	"God is *with* me <u>right now</u> as I do bad stuff to feel good. And He still loves me. He thinks that I am worth being there with me. He *wants* me to realize who I am so that I stop doing bad stuff. I will stop because Jesus loves me. I can be holy since *He is* holy."[13] (You can't 'lose' Jesus. He is right there whispering, "You don't have to do this. I love you.")

---

your body."

[12] 1 Corinthians 6:11 "But you were washed, you were sanctified, you were justified, in the name of the Lord Jesus Christ and by the Spirit of our God."

[13] 1 Peter 1:16 ". . . for it is written: 'Be holy, because I am holy.'"

The result?

Case	Old Way: Separated God	New Way: With God
Result:	Sin encourages sin.	Love encourages love.[14]

Be Free. Live in Jesus

Where would you put your relationship with God right now?

▲   ▲
Old Way: New Way:
Separated God   With God

What do you do if the 'old' thoughts come back? Tell them to get out of here![15] This is a fight for *your* spirit in the spiritual realm.[16] Cling to Jesus! Come to Jesus as children. Say, "Jesus, save me![17] Get me out of this! Show me how!" And then listen. Tell those bad thoughts, "In the name of Jesus get out of here!"[18]

Declare the truth as one who has accepted Christ's gift, "I am a saint, glorified, and child of God." Be a child. Cry out. God understands.[19] God *knows*. Submit to Him! Let Him be your boss! Listen to Him. Do as He tells you to align with His love.[20] You may

> **New; καινός; kainos:** Strong's 2537. Usage: fresh, unused, novel. Properly, new in quality, a transformation, superior to what was before — that's what you are in Christ!

---

[14] Galatians 5:16 "So I say, walk by the Spirit, and you will not gratify the desires of the flesh."

[15] Matthew 16:23 "Get behind Me, Satan! You are a stumbling block to Me. For you do not have in mind the things of God, but the things of men."

[16] James 4:7 "Submit yourselves, then, to God. Resist the devil, and he will flee from you."

[17] Matthew 14:30 "But when he saw the strength of the wind, he was afraid and, beginning to sink, cried out, 'Lord, save me!'"

[18] Acts 19:13 "Now there were some itinerant Jewish exorcists who tried to invoke the name of the Lord Jesus over those with evil spirits. They would say, 'I command you by Jesus, whom Paul proclaims.'"

[19] Mark 10:14 "Let the little children come to Me, and do not hinder them! For the kingdom of God belongs to such as these."

[20] Romans 9:30 "What then will we say? That Gentiles, not pursuing righteousness, have attained righteousness, and righteousness that *is* by faith; . . ."

feel like a lost coin[21] or a lost sheep[22] but He is not going to lose you. Take refuge in His goodness![23] Replace the old with holy pleasures overflowing[24] from God: praise, music and dance, real unadulterated food, God's nature, eye-contact conversations, sunshine, the Bible, thankfulness, and more!

God has Blessed You

God's blessings are already all around you.[25] Give thanks for His already overwhelming blessings while you experience His 'new' holy gifts, sing His 'new' song,[26] and enjoy the 'new' holy you living in union as the Trinity + You! Hallelujah!

A New Takeaway?

1. God's love relationship with us,
2. makes us new!
3. a new identity in Him,
4. which enables us to love others in a new way.

---

[21] Luke 15:9 "Rejoice with me, for I have found my lost coin."

[22] Luke 15:6 "Rejoice with me, for I have found my lost sheep!"

[23] Psalm 34:8 "Taste and see that the LORD is good; blessed is the man who takes refuge in Him!"

[24] Luke 6:38 "Give, and it will be given to you. A good measure, pressed down, shaken together, and running over will be poured into your lap."

[25] Mark 5:19 "'Go home to your own people,' He said, 'and tell them how much the Lord has done for you, and what mercy He has shown you.'"

[26] Psalm 40:3 "He put a new song in my mouth, a hymn of praise to our God."

13. Sin, Hamartia 266

Christians are surprised to find the Liar still tries to bait them, their body still has hungers, they cope using the same old tools, and that they do not-loving things. It looks like nothing has changed, but it has. Jesus Christ has conquered sin and has given Christians the power to conquer[1] sin through Him.

What does 'sin' mean to you?

      Evil   Naughty   Not-God

Definitions

An easy victory against the Liar is to agree on *who* defines 'good', 'evil', and 'sin'. Then we can use their definitions with no modification or debate.

Who can understand all situations and answer all questions with authority? God does. Humans try to modify God's definitions, but they all fall short of God's goodness and wisdom.[2]

Therefore, how does God define sin?

God = Love (1 John 4:16[3])

Sin = Not-God (1 John 3:5[4])

Sin = Not-Love

We know God is love, and Jesus did not sin.[5] Therefore sin is not-God and not-love. *Pause and digest — agree, disagree, or discuss?*

Not-love is *way bigger* than a simple list of sins. Not-love is every thought or action that doesn't flow from God and His love.[6]

---

[1] Romans 8:37 "No, in all these things we are more than conquerors through Him who loved us."

[2] Romans 3:23 ". . . for all have sinned and fall short of the glory of God, . . ."

[3] 1 John 4:16 "And we have come to know and believe the love that God has for us. God is love; whoever abides in love abides in God, and God in him."

[4] 1 John 3:5 "And you know that He appeared, so that He might take away sins; and in Him there is no sin."

[5] 1 Peter 2:22 "He committed no sin, and no deceit was found in His mouth."

[6] Romans 14:23 "But the one who has doubts is condemned if he eats, because his eating is not from faith; and everything that is not from faith is sin."

The result is simple. If it is not-love, it is not-God, which is sin. The action could be the same externally, but if your heart is away from God, it is not an action of love and not an action of God.[7]

When people talk about 'sin', the natural response is, "Well, I'm not a murderer. I'm doing OK." But with not-love being compared to God's level of love, we see we are <u>way</u> off the mark. In other words, you may not be a murder, but you exhibit not-love lots and lots.

What is not-love? It is the <u>not-fruit</u> of the Spirit of God. Have you ever exhibited:

- not-*love* being uncharitable, stingy, or just plain unpleasant at the expense of others?
- not-*joy* being negative to people's positive news?
- not-*peace* being chaotic around others?
- not-*patience* getting frustrated over things you shouldn't have?
- not-*kindness* taking pleasure in making someone feel bad?
- not-*goodness* to a coworker?
- not-*faithfulness* to a friend?
- not-*gentle* in touch to someone tender?
- not-*self-control* by being greedy or binging?

These are not-love, which is not-God, and therefore sin. Defining not-love this broadly helps us see our *true* life, our *true* need for God, and be astonished at the *true* greatness of God's love.[8]

What is the cure from all our not-love? God's love! Live in Christ! Live in His love! Move in His Holy Spirit! Share His divine nature as the Trinity + You![9]

Good to Bad Graph

God's goal for us is to avoid not-love,[10] not by *avoiding* it, but instead by *focusing* on the love of Jesus Christ. This way, our *focus* is

---

[7] Ezekiel 33:31 "So My people come to you as usual, sit before you, and hear your words; but they do not put them into practice. Although they express love with their mouths, their hearts pursue dishonest gain."

[8] Luke 9:43 "And they were all astonished at the greatness of God."

[9] 2 Peter 1:4 "Through these He has given us His precious and magnificent promises, so that through them you may become partakers of the divine nature, now that you have escaped the corruption in the world caused by evil desires."

[10] 1 John 3:4 "Everyone committing sin also commits lawlessness; and sin is lawlessness."

to have every thought and action flow through love, flow through Him.[11] By joining ourselves to Jesus Christ, in the Trinity + You union, we can live through Him.[12]

Let us explore the results of this definition by adding up all thoughts and actions that are love, neutral, and not-love of your week on a Good-to-Bad graph. Something like this:

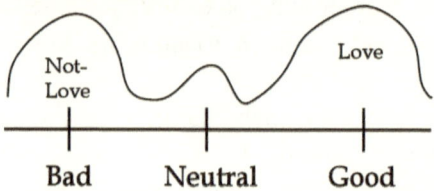

Draw what your graph would look like. Which of the three piles are the biggest? Would *others* agree with you? Would *God* agree with you? *Pause and digest — agree, disagree, or discuss?*

If you are angry, irritable, or have a general mood of not-love, when you talk to someone, not-love will contaminate that conversation.

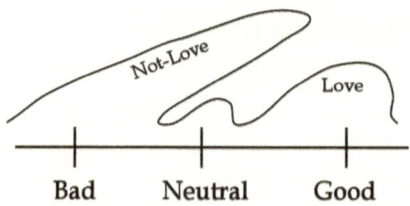

The author knows from his own and others' experience that our thoughts and actions can flow through love only *if* we live in Jesus Christ. Focusing on Christ, being in union as the Trinity + You, makes a graph where *love increases* and not-love decreases by practicing reliance on Him. *Pause and digest — agree, disagree, or discuss?*

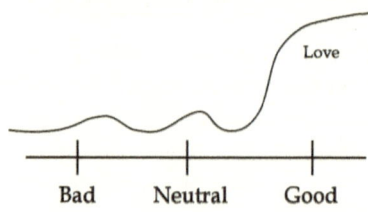

---

[11] Matthew 5:48 "Be [teleios; the end goal], therefore, as your heavenly Father is [teleios; the end goal]." (see Chapter 16 "Mature, Teleios 5046")

[12] 1 John 4:9 "This is how God's love was revealed among us: God sent His one and only Son into the world, so that we might live through Him."

A Guide for Everything

How should we satisfy our hungers? Be in-Christ, live in-love.[13]
How should we talk to people? Be in-Christ, live in-love.
How should we brush our teeth? Be in-Christ, live in-love.

It may seem silly to brush your teeth 'in-Christ', but did you flick spittle on the mirror? Did you leave a mess for someone else to clean up? If so, that was not-love (not-kindness and not-goodness!).

If we pay attention, we'll see that
most if not all of our lives are directly or indirectly love or not-love. How much of our actions are expressed through 100% neutrality? *Pause and digest — agree, disagree, or discuss?*

Do you leave shopping carts blocking the parking space or put them in the cart corral? Did you *compliment* the 99.9% great things about someone's work or nitpick the 0.1%? Do you share with others awful things or awe-inspiring things? Are you considered the fresh breeze of Christ[14] or a sour odor that people endure?

Jesus Christ has given all believers the power to conquer not-love by living though *His* love.[15]

> **Sin; ἁμαρτία; hamartia:**
> Strong's 266. Usage: missing the mark or the goal, rebellion, *everything* not of God (Romans 14:23). Does not matter if in error or deliberate, it is still 'not-love'.

One could write 1,000 Christian self-help books, but they would all be one page,[16] saying, "Walk in Love"![17]

How can you transform yourself? Be in-Christ, live in-love.
How can you overcome past hurts? Be in-Christ, live in-love.
How should we raise children? Be in-Christ, live in-love.
How to be a good manager? Be in-Christ, live in-love.
How do you 'grow rich'? Be in-Christ, live in-love (note: *His* riches are not piles of metal disks!).[18]

---

[13] John 15:12 "This is My commandment, that you love one another as I loved you."

[14] 2 Corinthians 2:15 "For we are to God the sweet aroma of Christ among those who are being saved and those who are perishing."

[15] Colossians 2:9 "For in Christ all the fullness of the Deity dwells in bodily form."

[16] Though *this* book isn't one page. Ha!

[17] Ephesians 5:2 ". . . and walk in love, just as Christ loved us and gave Himself up for us as a fragrant sacrificial offering to God."

[18] Proverbs 27:24 ". . . for riches are not forever, nor does a crown endure to every generation."

Be in-Christ, Live in-Love

But how *do we get* our hearts to constantly be in-Christ? There is no magic formula. It is *anything* that helps *you* stay focused on Christ and keep you grabbing on to the Holy Spirit for help:

- Start each day by bending your physical knee to the ground and saying out loud, "Not my will but yours, God."[19]
- Tune our electronics to better places that promote love.[20]
- Start each day reading a new verse, just one little line, and repeat it all day and any time you wake at night.
- Write an 'X' on your wrists[21] where Jesus was nailed to the cross, lifting you into glory.[22]
- Every hour give thanks to Christ for all that He has *already given you*, name *anything*, and see how your blessings upon blessing are *already* overwhelming.[23]
- Or rest in Jesus![24] Do-do nothing! Remember that Jesus loves you just as you were, just as you are, and just as you will be! How does that make you feel?

The list of possibilities goes on forever, as unique as the Trinity + You. To conquer not-love, flood your life *with* Christ to be in-Christ and live in-love.

How Then Shall We Live?

God is Love,
Focus on *His* love for you, so that
You can be in-Christ and live in-Love,
To love others as He loves you.

---

[19] Luke 22:42 "Yet not My will, but Yours be done."

[20] Colossians 3:2 "Set your minds on things above, not on earthly things."

[21] Galatians 6:17 "From now on let no one cause me trouble, for I bear on my body the marks of Jesus."

[22] Galatians 2:20 "I have been crucified with Christ, and I no longer live, but Christ lives in me. The life I live in the body, I live by faith in the Son of God, who loved me and gave Himself up for me."

[23] 2 Peter 1:3 "His divine power has given us everything we need for life and godliness through the knowledge of Him who called us by His own glory and excellence."

[24] Hebrews 4:11 "Let us, therefore, make every effort to enter that rest, so that no one will fall by following the same pattern of disobedience."

14. Excuse, Prophasis 4392

How does God expect us to live in a world of not-love? How are we to cope with the hurts in our life? Are physical needs a blessing or a curse? Does God provide excuse and or allowance to not-love?

What does 'excuse' mean?

▲   ▲

I have no choice   I have a choice and
                                                need to mature

There Is No Excuse to Sin

There is no excuse for not-love (sin).[1] There is *allowance* for not-love (sin) since God clearly understands that we *have* and *will* not-love — He took all of ours on to His body on the cross to heal us.[2]

Then how much power does sin have? None. That's right, none, except what you don't stamp out![3] You are free, 100% free.[4] Even with our past hurts and limited abilities we need to yearn for and pursue God's good fruit.

Therefore, there is no excuse to sin. There is allowance, but no excuse. *Pause and digest — agree, disagree, or discuss?*

God, who *is love,* gave us our physical world. His gifts to us, (such as food, physical bodies, wealth) can all be used for love or not-love. God intends His gifts *to be blessings* or else He would be a God of not-love. That makes no sense for God to give us bad fruit!

His blessings may feel like curses when:
1. We *stray* from God's definitions of the thing and God's intended use of it.
2. We are *maturing*, learning to be in Christ.
3. We are *healing*, learning to cope in Christ.
4. With a *bad heart* we yearn for things not of Christ.

---

[1] John 15:22 "If I had not come and spoken to them, they would not be guilty of sin. Now, however, they have no excuse for their sin."

[2] 1 Peter 2:24 "He Himself bore our sins in His body on the tree, so that we might die to sin and live to righteousness. 'By His stripes you are healed.'"

[3] Ephesians 6:16 "In addition to all this, take up the shield of faith, with which you can extinguish all the flaming arrows of the evil one."

[4] Romans 6:7 "For anyone who has died has been freed from sin."

Living more in Christ is a lifetime pursuit! He wants you to mature and has placed His Holy Spirit in you to make it possible.

Perspectives

Understanding the *source* of not-love helps us mature. Not-love loses its hold on us when we see it as part of the *natural process* to maturity. No parent watching a toddler learning how to walk would scream out, "Stop falling! Stop it! Just don't fall!" The parent has *allowance* for the toddler to stumble, learn, and mature.

Excuse; πρόφασις; prophasis: Strong's 4392. A 'front' (pro) 'appearance' (phasis). Used to describe insincere justification, a false appearance or reason, covering true intent, like 'putting on a show' in Luke 20:47. Do *you* ever do this to cover your not-love?

Then why *do* we stumble?[5] We may choose things not realizing they are not-love. Or, not-love *was* our 'normal', when *now* it is *not*! Old habits, old experiences, the Liar nagging us, these things are like thinking of cucumbers[6] in Egypt when we have something even better now. Don't give them root! Don't feed them! The birds circle above but don't build them a nest![7] We have *Christ in us* to shout to these wrong voices, "That's not me!" How can we even think of going back to the old ways, with our belly as our god,[8] when the old ways didn't make us happy?[9]

Growing in Christ takes time to see your true identity in Christ. *Live* like your true identity in Christ,[10] *grow* in the power of your true identity in Christ,[11] and your stumbling will be less and less.

---

[5] James 3:2 "We all stumble in many ways."

[6] Numbers 11:5 "We remember the fish we ate freely in Egypt, along with the cucumbers, melons, leeks, onions, and garlic."

[7] *Explanation of the Lord's Prayer*, Martin Luther, Sixth Petition of "And lead us not into temptation"), paragraph 161 (Included in Book *Luther's Catechetical Writings: God's Call To Repentance, Faith And Prayer* edited by John Nicholas Lenker, Vol. 1, 1907, pdf online public domain).

[8] Philippians 3:19 "Their end is destruction, their god is their belly, and their glory is in their shame. Their minds are set on earthly things."

[9] Romans 6:2 "Never may it be! How shall we who died to sin still live in it?"

[10] 2 Peter 1:10, referring to 5-9 "For if you practice these things you will never stumble, . . ."

[11] Jude 1:24 "Now to Him who is able to keep you from stumbling and to present you unblemished in His glorious presence, . . ."

Understanding the *cause* of our not-love is *not a license to* not-love.[12] It is to put not-love in God's perspective, remove the guilt and fear, and encourage growth.

Straying — From God's Definitions

The Liar wants 'good' to be called 'bad' and 'bad' to be called 'good'. They are not his to define. God gave us good pleasures to be used in good ways, His ways! God gave us boundaries and definitions to satisfy our mechanical needs in ways that avoid not-love. The Liar tries to confuse God's boundaries and definitions to trick people into guilt and doing more not-love.

Caution! Where are you getting guidance from? Other humans? The Liar's media? Or God?[13]

Hint — if you have questions, ask God! Search His word! Keep asking Him[14] until you know His truth. God will provide you wisdom, knowledge, and understanding.[15] Jesus and the Holy Spirit came for this very purpose. Your union in the Trinity + You relationship is the key. *Pause and digest — agree, disagree, or discuss?*

Maturing — Learning to Be in Christ

Quick, unintentional acts of not-love are *expected* as we learn to be every moment in Christ, living in-tune and in synch with the Holy Spirit.

One may have said something stupid,[16] or weren't paying attention properly, or pre-Christian habits popped out. God makes allowance for these, but there should be less repeats over time. Like children, we need to learn and mature in our self-control.[17] This includes managing our physical self (sleep, sustenance, activities) to help succeed in our spiritual self.

---

[12] 1 Corinthians 6:12 "'Everything is permissible for me,' but not everything is beneficial. 'Everything is permissible for me,' but I will not be mastered by anything."

[13] Psalm 37:3 "Trust in the LORD and do good; dwell in the land and cultivate faithfulness."

[14] Luke 11:8 "I tell you, even though he will not get up to provide for him because of his friendship, yet because of the man's persistence, he will get up and give him as much as he needs."

[15] Proverbs 2:6 "For the LORD gives wisdom; from His mouth come knowledge and understanding."

[16] Ephesians 5:4 "Nor should there be obscenity, foolish talk, or crude joking, which are out of character, but rather thanksgiving."

[17] 2 Peter 1:6 ". . . and to knowledge, self-control; and to self-control, perseverance; and to perseverance, godliness; . . ."

When these mess-ups happen, own it. Humbly confess your not-loving act and heal the relationship.[18] Try to restore any damage done and work in Christ to *prevent* the circumstances and results from happening again. Continue to be in-tune to other's needs, which is the Trinity + You love. *Pause and digest — agree, disagree, or discuss?*

Healing — Coping and Healing from Deep Hurts

Coping with hurts are like the hidden box of roaches in our soul; no one wants to talk about them, they are slow to come out, and tough to squish.

Humans learn to cope by surviving life. We can and do survive deep, scarring hurts which research shows happen way too often.[19] Coping skills can be learned from others or created out of necessity. They can be not-loving to yourself or others.

Should this author throw a stone to condemn the traumatized veteran who passes out drunk to sleep past the explosive sounds from Fourth of July fireworks? No. Nor can this author judge the child-abused adult that has trouble trusting. Will a just God condemn them? Of course not. God knows your hurts, and knows when you reach to Him you are doing your best.

God is *not* mad at you. God *made you* so He knows your needs. God *knows you* so knows all your hurts and coping skills.[20] God knows your heart, so knows how to help you get back to success with Him, through Jesus Christ and the Holy Spirit, as we submit ourselves in the Trinity + You union.

What makes human relationships difficult is that a person doing not-loving coping reactions may be very loving apart from the problem situation, and may not understand why they react the way they did or what triggered them.[21]

Coping with deep hurts has the most allowance for not-love as it is the *hardest* to understand and change. But know this — Jesus Christ <u>can</u>

---

[18] James 5:16 "Therefore confess your sins to each other and pray for each other so that you may be healed."

[19] There are many troubling statistics in this heavy, sad book that is helping healing: *The Body Keeps the Score: Brain, Mind, and Body in the Healing of Trauma* by Bessel van der Kolk M.D.

[20] Psalm 139:1 "For the choirmaster. A Psalm of David. O LORD, You have searched me and known me."

[21] One study showed 38% of adult participants did not recall the documented abuse that occurred against them when they were children. *The Body Keeps the Score*, Chap. 12, Sec. "The Science of Repressed Memory".

and does help you kill these roaches from your past. It may take days or decades but Christ is *with you* every step of the way to get to a better place of living.

While there may be allowance for not-love coping, there is still no excuse to *stay* as you are when God has a fuller life for you through Jesus Christ.[22]

Admit your feelings to Christ and run into His arms.[23] Pray to God for greater understanding of ourselves and others. Pray for compassion. Pray for healing. Pray that the coping tools become as positive as possible. Pray for wisdom to take the actions you need in body, spirit, and mind.[24] Listen and submit to the Holy Spirit guiding you into His perfect love for you. While you may not notice the change of season in your spirit, know that God is bringing forth the tender leaves of change.[25] *Pause and digest — agree, disagree, or discuss?*

Bad Heart — Yearning for Things Not of Christ

A bad heart is when we yearn for things not of Christ. You want to not-love so you do it. Slow, deliberate, nurtured, desire to not-love.[26] God is in your heart talking to you, but we always have free-choice to listen or not. Good or bad, what you want owns your heart.[27]

Let's be real. The seeds you plant grow.[28] We get to choose our attention: the rhythm of the Holy Spirit or the Liar's deceptions.[29] Where we focus our time, by thought and deed, becomes who we are.

A bad heart has the least allowance. You wanted it. You worked to do it. What are you going to do about it? *Pause and digest — agree, disagree, or discuss?*

---

[22] John 10:10 "I have come that they may have life, and have it in all its fullness."

[23] Mark 10:16 "And He took the children in His arms, placed His hands on them, and blessed them."

[24] 1 Corinthians 14:15 "What then shall I do? I will pray with my spirit, but I will also pray with my mind. I will sing with my spirit, but I will also sing with my mind."

[25] Matthew 24:32 "Now learn this lesson from the fig tree: As soon as its branches become tender and sprout leaves, you know that summer is near."

[26] James 1:15 "Then after desire has conceived, it gives birth to sin; and sin, when it is full-grown, gives birth to death."

[27] Luke 12:34 "For where your treasure is, there your heart will be also."

[28] Galatians 6:7 "Do not be deceived: God is not to be mocked. Whatever a man sows, he will reap in return."

[29] Romans 8:5 "For those being according to flesh mind the things of the flesh; but those according to Spirit, the things of the Spirit."

When Mess-Ups Happen

Good News! You are not Jesus! You are allowed to mess-up! *When these mess-ups happen, our response is the same. Join in union with the Trinity and act in love*:

1. Now Own It: With God, talk to Him about the situation to open your mind to His mind.[30]
2. Past: Apologize to those affected, admitting faults keeps us humble.[31]
3. Present: Restore, putting things back the way they were before the mess-up as best you can, is *just*.[32]
4. Future: Prevent future occurrence, learn and mature.[33]
5. Continue: Love in-tune with the Trinity and others daily as our new spiritual self.[34]

Pause and digest — agree, disagree, or discuss?

Back on Track

Yes, Jesus died once for all of your not-love acts. Yes, you are forgiven for always. But now you've tasted the glory of God[35] and still choose dog vomit?[36] Let us live in the light![37]

The good news is a mistake does not make your *identity*. A mistake is something you did; your identity is who you are — a child of God.[38] The cure for mistakes are quick and simple: submit to Christ. Bow your heart to Him. Get off your spiritual high horse and let God have the reins to reign!

You still have to try to restore what you made wrong, as best you can. Humble yourself with an apology to God ("I was wrong to ___ and

---

[30] A changed mind is metanoeó 3340. (See Chapter 22 "Repent, Metanoeó 3340")

[31] Matthew 23:11 "But the greatest among you will be your servant."

[32] Isaiah 61:8 "For I, the LORD, love justice; I hate robbery and iniquity; in My faithfulness I will give them their recompense and make an everlasting covenant with them."

[33] 1 Corinthians 14:20 "Brothers, stop thinking like children. In regard to evil be infants, but in your thinking be mature."

[34] Luke 9:23 "Then Jesus said to all of them, 'If anyone wants to come after Me, he must deny [the old] and take up his [new saving love] daily and follow Me.'"

[35] 1 Peter 2:3 "... now that you have tasted that the Lord is good."

[36] 2 Peter 2:22 "Of them the proverbs are true: 'A dog returns to its vomit,' and, 'A sow that is washed goes back to her wallowing in the mud.'"

[37] 2 Peter 3:1 "Both of them are reminders to stir you to [judge by light] thinking..."

[38] Romans 8:16 "The Spirit Himself testifies with our spirit that we are God's children."

thank you for already forgiving me") and an apology to those you have hurt. Prevent anything that would place you heading back in that direction again. Continue to tune-in to the love of Jesus.

Don't allow *even the dust* of darkness to mix with the light of Jesus Christ. How much turd will you allow in the brownies you eat? A log just on Friday night? A nugget every now and then? A couple of flakes? Do not allow even *the dust* of turd in your brownies. Get it out! Out! That is *not* you anymore. You are the temple of God walking in this world. You are as pure as Jesus is pure.[39] You are the lamp of God's light.[40] <u>Live like it.</u> Pause and digest — agree, disagree, or discuss?

These descriptions are not intended to condemn. They are to help you walk as valuable as Christ made you.[41] God still loves you *and likes you!*

As disciples of Jesus we need to continue to mature. These descriptions are to help understand the *reasons* behind our behavior which then gives us allowance *to mature* into more and more victories through Jesus Christ our Lord and Savior.[42] Learning *processes* to get back on track when not-love occurs, from the love of a Trinity + You union, makes the maturity easier and faster. If the process before didn't stick, try this repackaging —

> OARPL
> O: Own It; talk with God about it.
> A: Apologize to those affected.
> R: Restore things as best possible.
> P: Prevent the circumstances.
> L: Love continually as the Trinity + You.

Can We Distill This Chapter More?

God has freed you by His Love,
Continue to mature in <u>His</u> love, so that
<u>You</u> increase love for others, humbly, continually,
As you and they are able,
As He loves you.

---

[39] 1 John 3:3 "And everyone who has this hope in Him purifies himself, just as Christ is pure."
[40] Matthew 5:14 "You are the light of the world. A city on a hill cannot be hidden."
[41] Ephesians 4:1 "As a prisoner in the Lord, then, I urge you to walk in a manner worthy of the calling you have received . . ."
[42] 2 Peter 3:18 "But grow in the grace and knowledge of our Lord and Savior Jesus Christ."

15. Light, Phós 5457

A Christian challenges:
"I'm new in Christ and 'free' from sin. Life should be great but mine stinks like turd. Isn't life supposed to be filled with the light of goodness, righteousness, and truth?[1] Why isn't mine?"

What is your life filled with?

▲ Worldly Darkness   ▲ Godly Light

Freedom to Have Life to the Max

New and old Christians are surprised to find they still have free-choice, that the Liar is still active, and that staying nice takes work. Luke teaches that God is not controlling your life choices.[2] Life is a free *choice* between light and dark every moment of every day. *Pause and digest — agree, disagree, or discuss?*

Mathematically, Life is the summation of all positive Light and negative Dark:

Life = $\sum$ (Light − Dark)

To maximize our Life, 'life to the max' or $\text{Life}_{(max)}$, Light must increase while Dark goes to zero. Jesus is Light with zero Dark.[3] Therefore, $\text{Life}_{(max)}$ is filled entirely with Jesus.[4]

Mathematically:

$\text{Life}_{(max)} = \sum$ (Jesus)

How do we fill our life entirely with Jesus? Turn *to* Jesus and *away* from not-Jesus.[5] Or, turn to Love and away from not-Love. When the

---

[1] Ephesians 5:9 "... for the fruit of the light consists in all goodness, righteousness, and truth."

[2] Luke 11:35 "Your eye is the lamp of your body. When your eye is clear, your whole body is also light; but when it is evil, your body is also dark."

[3] John 8:12 "Once again, Jesus spoke to the people and said, 'I am the light of the world. Whoever follows Me will never walk in the darkness, but will have the light of life.'"

[4] Colossians 1:9 "... asking God to fill you with the knowledge of His will in all spiritual wisdom and understanding..."

[5] Acts 26:18 "... to open their eyes, so that they may turn from darkness to light and from the power of Satan to God, that they may receive forgiveness of sins and an

Liar of this world shoves darkness in your face or serenades you with darkness, turn away from it and turn to Jesus.[6] Turn to whatever God has made pure, lovely, and right.[7]

How? "Turn to Jesus," is easy to say, and harder to do. Simply replace any bad fruit with good fruit. You can't be filled with both light and dark at the same time. Light and dark don't mix.[8] The simple process to have life in abundance,[9] Life$_{(max)}$, is to fill your eyes, ears, mouth, hands, and mind with Godly things, which is the same as God's light.

Look at your life right now. What do you fill it with? What do you spend time thinking about? What are the results of your pursuits?

Fill Up with Jesus's Light

If Jesus is the light that shines into us,[10] and we are His jewel,[11] then we have free-choice decisions to make every moment of every day. We could turn 100% *away* from Jesus[12] *to* darkness, and His light will <u>100% reflect</u> off of us. We can turn *some* of the way to Him, so *some* of His light reflects off, but some flows through us radiating out His love to

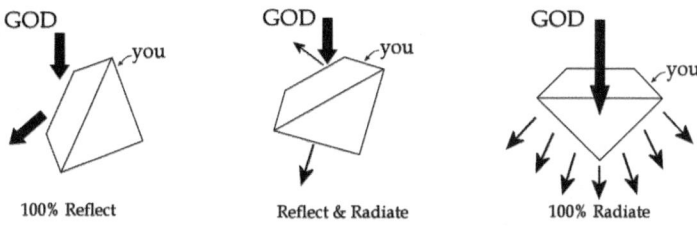

inheritance among those sanctified by faith in Me."

[6] Isaiah 55:7 "Let the wicked man forsake his way and the unrighteous man his thoughts; let him return to the LORD, that He may have compassion, and to our God, for He will freely pardon."

[7] Philippians 4:8 "Finally, brothers, whatever is true, whatever is honorable, whatever is right, whatever is pure, whatever is lovely, whatever is admirable—if anything is excellent or praiseworthy—think on these things."

[8] Ephesians 5:11 "Have no fellowship with the fruitless deeds of darkness, but rather expose them."

[9] John 10:10 "I came that they may have life, and may have it abundantly."

[10] 2 Corinthians 4:6 "For God, who said, 'Let light shine out of darkness,' made His light shine in our hearts to give us the light of the knowledge of the glory of God in the face of Jesus Christ."

[11] Zechariah 9:16 "On that day the LORD their God will save them as the flock of His people; for like jewels in a crown they will sparkle over His land."

[12] Galatians 1:6 "I am amazed how quickly you are deserting the One who called you by the grace of Christ and are turning to a different gospel—"

others. Best yet, we can turn 100% *to Him* so that His light fills us to overflowing, so much so that we 100% radiate *His* light out to others.[13]

> **Light, φῶς phós:**
> Strong's 5457. Usage: To shine or make clear, illuminate the truth, or a symbol for God (pillar of fire) or His goodness.

The only light we can shine in the world is *from Him*. It's our free-choice to accept it. Letting "your light shine before men" is radiating *His* light. Isn't that a relief? It's not your burden to do-do God's works, it's His! A nuance, but a very important one, that people confuse which has a significant difference in results. *Pause and digest — agree, disagree, or discuss?*

Living in this world we are surrounded by darkness. It is easy to spend hours gobbling it up. Regardless if you respond to this darkness with worry, anger, or glee,[14] you are still filling up on darkness instead of the light of Jesus.

How much of your time, energy, or focus is spent on:[15]

- Idols at work
- Hate in politics
- Jealousy of worldly things
- Not-love thinking
- Dividing people
- And similar fruits of the flesh?

All of these are *not* the Holy Fruit of the *Spirit*. How much time is spent with Him or His Holy Fruit? No wonder why people are stressed out and missing the peace of Christ![16]

The Parable of the Turd

Some may say we *should* focus on sin, not-love, darkness and evil to combat it. That may be true, but it is shameful[17] that not-love often gets *way more attention* than love, darkness more attention than light.

---

[13] Matthew 5:16 "In the same way, let your light shine before men, that they may see your good deeds and glorify your Father in heaven."

[14] John 3:19 "And this is the verdict: The Light has come into the world, but men loved the darkness rather than the Light because their deeds were evil."

[15] Galatians 5:20 "... idolatry and sorcery; hatred, discord, jealousy, and rage; rivalries, divisions, factions ..."

[16] 2 Peter 1:2 "Grace and peace be multiplied to you through the knowledge of God and of Jesus our Lord."

[17] Ephesians 5:12 "For it is shameful even to mention what the disobedient do in secret."

Being sin focused is like being turd focused:

"Did you see their stinky turd? And her? She turds all the time. Praise the Lord I don't have big turds like them.[18] They're just doing the same turds as on TV! Nothing but turd after turd. Turds on every channel. And the turds in the world today! Everywhere you go, turds, turds, turds! People love their turds! But not me."

And what are *you* thinking about *now*? It is *not* the Holy Spirit. That's what happens when we turn away from God's pure creation. Life stinks! *Pause and digest — agree, disagree, or discuss?*

Live in His Light

To have the power and peace of Christ rule in us,[19] we must live in the pure light of Christ. If we keep turning our jewel to maximize His light in us, our lives will *glow* with the Trinity + You union. Being 'in Christ' makes us fully alive.[20] Darkness-avoidance will automatically occur when we *focus on Christ's light*. Life to the max, Life$_{(max)}$, is life in Christ.

The test to know if you are successfully living in the light is that your *public and private life are the same.* No hiding. Everything you would do in the private dark when no one is watching should also be able to be done in the public light for the world to see.[21] God sees it anyway!

Anything that God made you to do, do it in God's way which produces His good fruit.

Pause and digest — agree, disagree, or discuss?

---

[18] Luke 18:11 "The Pharisee stood by himself and prayed, 'God, I thank You that I am not like other men—swindlers, evildoers, adulterers—or even like this tax collector.'"

[19] Colossians 3:15 "Let the peace of Christ rule in your hearts, for to this you were called as members of one body. And be thankful."

[20] 1 Corinthians 15:22 "For as in Adam all die, so in Christ all will be made alive."

[21] Luke 8:17 "For there is nothing hidden that will not be disclosed, and nothing concealed that will not be made known and brought to light."

Summed Up

Live in the light.[22] You are the light of the Lord.[23] God wants to fill you with His light[24] to extinguish darkness in this world.[25]

Will you turn more to Him? You accepted Him. You have His everlasting light.[26] Your union could be greater. Your peace and power overflowing. [27] Fill your life with Jesus Christ.[28]

What Does This Mean for Us?

Keeping our lives filled with Jesus Christ,
Allows us to love others,
By filling us with His love
His love overflows to others.

---

[22] John 3:21 "But whoever practices the truth comes into the Light, so that it may be seen clearly that what he has done has been accomplished in God."

[23] Ephesians 5:8 "For you were once darkness, but now you are light in the Lord. Walk as children of light."

[24] Revelation 22:5 "And there will be no night there, and they have no need of the light of a lamp and of the light of the sun, because the Lord God will enlighten [illuminate (phótizó 5461)] them, and they will reign to the ages of the ages."

[25] John 1:5 "The Light shines in the darkness, and the darkness has not overcome it."

[26] Isaiah 60:20 "Your sun will no longer set, and your moon will not wane; for the LORD will be your everlasting light, and the days of your sorrow will cease."

[27] Romans 15:13 "Now may the God of hope fill you with all joy and peace as you believe in Him, so that you may overflow with hope by the power of the Holy Spirit."

[28] Ephesians 3:19 "... of the love of Christ, and to know this love that surpasses knowledge, that you may be filled with all the fullness of God."

16. Mature, Teleios 5046

Your salvation is perfected[1] from the moment you accept Jesus Christ as Lord of your life, but is your spiritual wisdom static? Of course not. We are to mature (teleios, 'the end goal') in Christ.[2] How then do we <u>mature</u>? We mature by every moment sorting and choosing Christ's righteousness.[3]

How filled is your life with Christ?

▲   ▲   ▲

When I need a favor   Christ at Christmas   Christ every moment

What is 'Maturing'?

Does being a Christian *longer* create maturity? Young Elihu says, "not always."[4] Just surviving the days doesn't help — listening to God helps![5]

Do we ever reach 'final' maturity where we do everything right? Of course not, so remove the guilt. Paul didn't either.[6]

Who can teach us right from wrong? The Holy Spirit does in your real life right now (if you ask Him!).[7] Maturing is then a *journey* of spiritual transformation, continually replacing worldly habits and reactions with *spiritual* habits and reactions taught to us from Jesus Christ.[8]

---

[1] Hebrews 10:14 "For by one offering, He has perfected (teleioó 5048, from teleios) for all time those being sanctified."

[2] Ephesians 4:13 ". . . until we all reach unity in the faith and in the knowledge of the Son of God, as we mature to the full measure of the stature of Christ."

[3] Hebrews 5:14 "But solid food is for the mature, who by constant use have trained their senses to distinguish good from evil."

[4] Job 32:7 "I thought that age should speak, and many years should teach wisdom."

[5] Job 32:8 "But there is a spirit in a man, the breath of the Almighty, that gives him understanding."

[6] Philippians 3:12 "Not that I have already obtained all this, or have already been made perfect, but I press on to take hold of that for which Christ Jesus took hold of me."

[7] 1 Corinthians 2:6, 13 "But we speak wisdom among the mature, . . . in words taught by the Spirit, expressing spiritual truths in spiritual words."

[8] 1 Corinthians 3:1 "Brothers, I could not address you as spiritual, but as worldly— as infants in Christ."

Mature Through Christ

Since maturity comes from Christ speaking through the Holy Spirit in you, this means the 'do-do-works Christian' cannot mature by obeying the modern 'Pharisee Rulebook': mandatory Bible reading, worship team, small group leader, tithing or any do-do-work that comes from men.[9] Man can't increase your maturity — God does![10]

> **Mature; τέλειος; teleios:**
> Strong's 5046. The end goal. Signifies 'reaching the end lacking nothing', 'complete in all parts', or 'fully grown'.

These do-do-works create a dead life.[11] They are deceitfully empty.[12] We want a *living* life! A life *filled* with the *living* Christ!

A relationship with God *can* produce those works, but those works *won't* produce a maturing relationship with God. Living as the Trinity + You produces mercy,[13] righteousness, *and* maturity from the *relationship*, not from the works.

Also hindered in maturity are Christians choked by worries, controlled by stuff, and slaves to pleasure.[14] How can we mature filled with *that*? Again, the solution is to fill our lives *with Jesus* through our mature talk, thought, and decisions from our Trinity + You relationship.[15]

It is the classic do-do trap scenario. We want to please God, so do-do things *we think* God will like instead of asking God himself! Is God on top leading our life or are works? Is it more important to God to send money to Africa or show kindness to the clerks at the store or to have a relationship with Him?

---

[9] 1 Corinthians 3:3 "For where jealousy and strife are among you, are you not fleshly, and are walking according to man?"

[10] 1 Corinthians 3:7 "So neither he who plants nor he who waters is anything, but only God, who makes things grow."

[11] Hebrews 6:1 "Therefore let us leave the elementary teachings about Christ and go on to maturity, not laying again the foundation of repentance from dead works, and of faith in God."

[12] Colossians 2:8 "See to it that no one takes you captive through philosophy and empty deception, which are based on human tradition and the spiritual forces of the world rather than on Christ."

[13] Luke 10:37 "'The one who showed him mercy,' replied the expert in the law. Then Jesus told him, 'Go and do likewise.'"

[14] Luke 8:14 "The seeds that fell among the thorns are those who hear, but as they go on their way, they are choked by the worries, riches, and pleasures of this life, and their fruit does not mature."

[15] 1 Corinthians 13:11 "When I was a child, I talked like a child, I thought like a child, I reasoned like a child. When I became a man, I set aside childish ways."

God's better life for us is where *He* works us to maturity as the Trinity + You.[16] How? Just as you submitted to have Christ Jesus as your Lord, *continue to walk* with Him as your Lord.[17] *He* works us to maturity as we continue to yearn, reach, and tune-in to God. In our maturity with Him, we'll be in-tune with God and automatically outflow His love. *Pause and digest — agree, disagree, or discuss?*

Tune-in to God

As a visual example, if God is the perfect note of love, our lives may be 'in' or 'out' of tune with His perfect note.

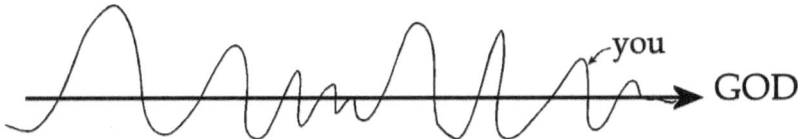

With our hearts yearning for God, we practice tuning-in our lives to Him and being in-synch with Him. Listening to His Holy Spirit in us and moving towards His perfect spiritual song, we naturally, without do-do-works, become one with Him — maturity! — and do His works (no matter how small or unglamourous wherever you are) as the Trinity + You. Notice again, that it is not sin-avoidance that makes us mature, it is tuning-in *to God* that makes us mature.

Asking, listening, and moving to the Holy Spirit's loving direction is the only way *possible* to live in harmony with the Lord.[18] Let His heartbeat be our heartbeat, so that our spiritual love will be woven from His spiritual love.[19] The good in you will come from Jesus.[20] The mystery of "Christ in you" will be fulfilled.[21] *Pause and digest — agree, disagree, or discuss?*

---

[16] Hebrews 11:40 "God had planned something better for us, so that together with us they would be made perfect (teleioó 5048)."

[17] Colossians 2:6 "Therefore, just as you have received Christ Jesus as Lord, continue to walk in Him, . . ."

[18] Colossians 3:14 "And over all these virtues put on love, which is the bond of perfect [maturity (teleiotés 5047)]."

[19] Colossians 2:2 ". . . that their hearts may be encouraged, having been knit together in love, and to all *the* riches of the full assurance of understanding, to *the* knowledge of the mystery of God, *which is* Christ, . . ."

[20] Philippians 2:13 "For it is God who works in you to will and to act on behalf of His good purpose."

[21] Colossians 1:27 "To them God has chosen to make known among the Gentiles the glorious riches of this mystery, which is Christ in you, the hope of glory."

And relax about your mess-ups. Humbly seek to restore things to the way they were before the mess-ups, learn from them, and stay living in the present as the Trinity + You. Maturity is a journey to get spiritually better every day. We all need practice in Christ, so be kind to yourself and be kind to others.[22]

Maturity in Summary

Maturity comes from living in union as the Trinity + You:
- God wants us to <u>mature</u>.[23]
- Maturity comes from <u>practice</u> tuning-in to God's way.[24]
- Practice builds <u>strength</u> to win the race.[25]
- Strength comes from <u>Jesus Christ</u>.[26]

Ask Jesus! Listen! Submit! In every moment!

What Is Another Way to Say It?

1. Relationship with the Trinity,
    leads to
2. Maturing in the Trinity,
    leads to
3. Expressing the Trinity + You.

---

[22] Ephesians 4:32 "Be kind and tenderhearted to one another, forgiving each other just as in Christ God forgave you."

[23] Ephesians 4:15 "Instead, speaking the truth in love, we will in all things grow up into Christ Himself, who is the head."

[24] James 1:4 "Allow perseverance to finish its work, so that you may be mature and complete, not lacking anything."

[25] 1 Corinthians 9:25 "Everyone who competes in the games trains with strict discipline. They do it for a crown that is perishable, but we do it for a crown that is imperishable."

[26] 1 Peter 5:10 "And after you have suffered for a little while, the God of all grace, who has called you to His eternal glory in Christ, will Himself restore you, secure you, strengthen you, and establish you."

17. Humble, Tapeinos 5011

Does God want you to be humble? Would He create a process where succeeding in 'holy living' makes you less humble? Muslims, Jews, Hindus, all want to do humble acts to tip the afterlife judgement points in their favor, or at least score more points than their neighbors. Are Christians the same? How do you know you are doing a good job being humble?

What does 'humble' mean to you?

▲
Ways to get afterlife points.

▲
Knowing our relationship to God and others.

Jesus Fulfills Every Dot of the Rules

By doing humble acts to gain afterlife points for Muslim, Jewish, Hindu, and some Christians, the rule-based process of doing humble acts to gain afterlife points, in any religion, leads to 'compare and compete'.

The rule-based *process* requires adherents to judge *themselves* if they are humble. How can the humble judge their own humbleness? They can't. They *must* judge themselves as *compared to* others around them. They get assurance of afterlife success if they are better than the *competition*, "I'm doing better than *them*, so I must be OK." Comparison and competition are the natural result of their rule-based *process*.

Another problem with this 'compare and compete' rule-based process is it is only as good as the culture (family, neighbor, country) that surrounds them. Is *that* culture humble? Is *that* culture good or bad? Someone in the 1942 German culture could judge themselves as succeeding in 'goodness' by saying, "Well, *I* haven't killed anyone." But is that true? Are they humble in that statement?

Who is the *real* judge? The real judge is the *rule maker*, the definer of 'good', Jesus Christ.[1] *Pause and digest — agree, disagree, or discuss?*

---

[1] Romans 10:3 "Because they were ignorant of God's righteousness and sought to

All rule-based religions, including Christianity, must use texts of *general* rules for *specific* circumstances. For rule-based followers, they must decide *how to act* based on these fixed, general rules. But when you add a Trinity + You relationship, Jesus Christ talking to you through the Holy Spirit inside of you, the rules are a *foundation,* a starting point, from which the Trinity can correct you,[2] or guide you, in love.[3]

Rule-based living is doomed to fail as there are not enough words in the world to cover every specific situation and circumstance.[4] Even if there *were* enough words, no one could read them all! Which leads many religious participants to guilt, insecurity, and frustration. In the participant's frustration, they make the *rules* more important than the *rule-maker*, the *action* more important than the *heart*. What other choice do they have in their process? *Pause and digest — agree, disagree, or discuss?*

Humble; ταπεινός; tapeinos:
Strong's 5011. Low. Describes the person who depends on the Lord rather than self. A new virtue which Jesus introduced.

A Trinity + You union is different. The Trinity guides you in *His love with the right heart* every moment and in every situation. Only true relationship Christianity — Jesus Christ 'in you' instead of rule-based scorecard — fulfills all the rules[5] *and* allows you to live humbly in everyday situations.

For example, what happens if there is no rule in the sacred text? What should humble people do in strange new moral dilemmas or complicated social impacts, like nuclear power or growing organs in petri dishes? For rule-based followers, these dilemmas of what is 'good' (without God)[6] begin never-ending arguments.

---

establish their own, they did not submit to God's righteousness."

[2] 2 Timothy 3:16 "Every Scripture *is* God-breathed (i.e. His Spirit [theos, 'God' and pneō, 'to breathe']) and profitable for instruction, for conviction, for correction, *and* for training in righteousness,

[3] 1 Corinthians 2:13 "And this is what we speak, not in words taught of human wisdom, but in those taught of the Spirit, communicating spiritual things by spiritual means."

[4] John 21:25 "There are many more things that Jesus did. If all of them were written down, I suppose that not even the world itself would have space for the books that would be written."

[5] Matthew 5:17 "Do not think that I have come to abolish the Law or the Prophets. I have not come to abolish them, but to fulfill them."

[6] 1 Timothy 6:4 "... he is conceited and understands nothing. Instead, he has an unhealthy interest in controversies and semantics, out of which come envy, strife, abusive talk, evil suspicions, . . ."

Again, the better answer is Jesus Christ in you, as union of the Trinity + You,[7] fulfilling the *rule of love* and Him showing you the correct humble path of *His love through you* in all your life interactions.

Each rule-based religious person pursuing a better afterlife agrees to follow their process, acts based on their process, and so their process outcome is *fixed*. The rule-based Muslim, Jew, Hindu, and Christian take their humble acts, compare them to others, and compete with others, to judge if they are good 'enough' by being better than 'them'. Their process is a competition. The competition requires comparing. Comparing leads to pride. How often do we do the same? Do you see the escape? *Pause and digest — agree, disagree, or discuss?*

God's goal is for you to humble yourself so He can love you. God does not want growth in self-pride.[8] Would the perfect designer design a process that grows people *away* from His goal? Would He make your *success* the path to your failure? Would He make a humbleness competition that leads to pride? Of course not! That makes no sense.

Real Trinity + You relationship Christianity *is* different. God says you can *never do-do* good enough or be humble enough for a better afterlife. He *wants* you to give up trying to *do-do* it yourself and rely *on Him*.[9] You couldn't save yourself before accepting Jesus Christ as Lord of your life, and you still need Him after! His Holy Spirit in us is how we are rebirthed in Him.[10] This is the purpose of the Trinity + You union, joining ourselves to *Him* to become of *Him*.

Rely on Jesus

That is *why* God does not like self-pride. Self-pride makes us rely on *ourselves* instead of *Jesus Christ*. Self-pride reduces our love for Him and others. Self-pride thinks ourselves as 'better than them'[11] and makes 'why can't they' statements.

God wants us to be humble. He wants us to rely on Him. He wants *increased* love relationship for Him and others. Our good God has

---

[7] 2 Corinthians 13:14 "The grace of the Lord Jesus Christ, and the love of God, and the fellowship of the Holy Spirit be with all of you."

[8] James 4:6 "But He gives us more grace. This is why it says: 'God opposes the proud, but gives grace to the humble.'"

[9] Proverbs 3:5 "Trust in the LORD with all your heart, and lean not on your own understanding . . ."

[10] Titus 3:5 "He saved us, not by works in righteousness that we did, but according to His mercy, through *the* washing of regeneration and renewing of *the* Holy Spirit, . . ."

[11] Luke 18:11 "The Pharisee stood by himself and prayed, 'God, I thank You that I am not like the other men—swindlers, evildoers, adulterers—or even like this tax collector.'"

designed the process so success in one area increases success in all others. *Pause and digest — agree, disagree, or discuss?*

What process has God given us in relationship Christianity to achieve these results? What process, unique to relationship Christianity among all religions, leads to being humble?

- Bow our heart to Jesus Christ
- Admit He is Lord
- Live like it.

The Trinity + You relationship process makes us see and admit we are not good enough, and with all our good works can *never* be good enough![12] That's why we need Jesus — always!

God's love levels the playing field. We're all the same 'goodness' when compared to God.[13] The caste system, the arguments over the list of rules, the jealous neighbor put-downs, these all disappear when we humble ourselves to God's design by relying on Jesus Christ.

We All Need Jesus

We all need Jesus to lift us up.[14] *His* goodness saves us. *His* goodness shows us *how* to live by living *through* Him. His Holy Spirit guides us through any dilemma, no matter how new or complicated.

Knowing we humans are all at the same level when *compared to God*, knowing we can't be better than our neighbor, father, mother, brother, spouse — *knowing this* changes our relationship to *them*. We are humbled. We are all equal.[15] Instead of 'competing and comparing', we are humble. In humility we are able share the gifts that God gives each of us.[16]

As we judge ourselves, we'll judge others.[17] Do we judge with law or love? Are we *trying* to be 'good enough', or are we submitting to Jesus Christ to live through Him? Are we listening[18] for His direction and asking for His help? If you are, then *you don't need to judge* how

---

[12] Romans 3:10 "As it is written: 'There is no one righteous, not even one.'"

[13] Galatians 3:28 "There is neither Jew nor Greek, slave nor free, male nor female, for you are all one in Christ Jesus."

[14] James 4:10 "Humble yourselves before the Lord, and He will exalt you."

[15] Romans 2:11 "For God does not show favoritism."

[16] 1 Peter 4:10 "As good stewards of the manifold grace of God, each of you should use whatever gift he has received to serve one another."

[17] Luke 6:37 "Do not judge, and you will not be judged. Do not condemn, and you will not be condemned. Forgive, and you will be forgiven."

[18] Mark 4:33 "And with many such parables He kept speaking the word to them, as they were able to hear."

'good' you are or how 'good' anyone else is when Jesus is living *His* perfect 'good' through all of us! *Pause and digest — agree, disagree, or discuss?*

God's love makes us equal.[19] No person is better than another. God's process, submitting to Jesus Christ, forces us to be humble. Union with God, the Trinity + You, leads to *true* goodness, true Godliness, and true life. *He* is the only way.[20]

How Then Shall We Live?

God is Love,
Submit to <u>His</u> love, so that
<u>You</u> can love others,
Humbly, as He loves you.

---

[19] Acts 10:34 "Then Peter began to speak: 'I now truly understand that God does not show favoritism, . . .'"

[20] Matthew 7:14 "But small is the gate and narrow the way that leads to life, and only a few find it."

18. Word, Logos 3056

How do we go from knowing <u>about</u> Jesus to <u>knowing</u> Jesus? Go from living with the Bible as 'information' to actually <u>living</u> as the Trinity + You, today, right now?[1]

Are all Bible translations good? Is the Bible full of errors or missing books? Can we even trust it? And do I really have to read the book of Job?

How often should we read the Bible?

▲ | ▲ | ▲
Never; live in the Spirit. | Once per year | Mandatory daily

Answer

The answer is none of these (sorry, this is a trick question). The real answer to "How often we should read the Bible" is, 'as much as your heart yearns for it.' "Mandatory" Bible reading is a man-made <u>law</u>, not from God, full of the Liar's guilt when not 'checked off'. But to live in the Spirit without concrete guidance is downright dangerous.[2]

To live tuned-in to God, we therefore need the <u>fixed</u> word of God (the Bible[3]) and the <u>living</u> word of God (Jesus[4]). Both are complimentary;[5] the fixed word is interpreted <u>through</u> the living word (Jesus's love; hint — love is most important).

Here is a quick example. The fixed word (Bible) says to 'be gentle', right?[6] If you were just walking down the street and met this author, and suddenly this author screamed and shoved you hard into a scratchy

---

[1] James 1:22 "But be doers of *the* word, and not hearers only, deceiving yourselves."

[2] 1 John 4:1 "Beloved, do not believe every spirit, but test the spirits to see whether they are from God. For many false prophets have gone out into the world."

[3] Psalm 119:89 "Your word, O LORD, is everlasting; it is firmly fixed in the heavens."

[4] Hebrews 4:12 "For the word of God is living and active. Sharper than any double-edged sword, it pierces even to dividing soul and spirit, joints and marrow. It judges the thoughts and intentions of the heart."

[5] Matthew 22:29 "Jesus answered, 'You are mistaken because you do not know the Scriptures or the power of God.'"

[6] Philippians 4:5 "Let your gentleness be apparent to all. The Lord is near."

bush, this author was not aligned to the fixed word (the author wasn't 'gentle'). But if this author's actions saved you from getting hit by a bus, the living word (Jesus said, 'show compassion'[7]) trumped the fixed word ('be gentle'). Hence, we need both the fixed word interpreted through the living word (Jesus's love) to know how to live best in each moment. *Pause and digest — agree, disagree, or discuss?*

What is the Bible?

Those that actually knew Jesus created a fixed record (new testimonies) of how Jesus lived and how we should relate to God through Jesus Christ.[8] These followers also proved how Jesus, as the living Word (logos, concept that forces change), fulfills promises recorded by His earlier prophets in their old testimonies.[9]

Gathered together as 'The Bible', these old and new fixed testimonies describe God's old and new relationship methods[10] (old and new Testaments).[11]

Though God's relationship *method* adapted over time, His *desire to have relationship* with you and me is the *same* today as it was from *before the creation*.[12] Amazing? Yes! He wants a relationship with you and me![13] *Pause and digest — agree, disagree, or discuss?*

---

[7] Luke 10:33 "But a Samaritan on a journey came upon him, and when he saw him, he had compassion."

[8] Hebrews 12:2 "Let us fix our eyes on Jesus, the author and perfecter of our faith, who for the joy set before Him endured the cross, scorning its shame, and sat down at the right hand of the throne of God."

[9] Hebrews 1:1 "On many past occasions and in many different ways, God spoke to our fathers through the prophets."

[10] Hebrews 8:7 "For if that first covenant had been without fault, no place would have been sought for a second."

[11] English words 'Testimony' and 'Testament' are from the *same* Latin 'testis' (witness), but the biblical Greek root words are slightly different: Testament (diathéké: declaration *post death*) vs Testimony (martureó: declaration as a *living* witness). The significance is God's new covenant promise takes affect after the death and resurrection of Jesus Christ, as Hebrews 9:16 reemphasizes, as does a legal will.

[12] Matthew 25:34 "Then the King will say to those on His right, 'Come, you who are blessed by My Father, inherit the kingdom prepared for you from the foundation of the world.'"

[13] Psalm 8:4 ". . . what is man that You are mindful of him, or the son of man that You care for him?"

The Bible Is True

The Bible records the truth. It *can* be trusted.[14] For anyone that looks into it, and good Christianity encourages this, it is clear that the Bible has been God's fixed logos (word, idea, message) from the time it was originally written down by the people that *actually experienced Jesus* to us today.

> **Word; λόγος; logos:**
> Strong's 3056. Broad usage varies: Word, speech, message, account, doctrine, and expression of a thing. But more than that, it is a relationship through thought; communication.

Still, people claim the Bible is full of errors or is missing books. If the details are too similar or too different, they yell, "Fraud!" (Is there a perfect amount?) If there are 5,600[15] copies in the original Greek that match our Bible today, they demand more. (Is there ever enough?) Or they claim the testimonies are a conspiracy, failing to answer why groups of people would get together to create fables that would get themselves stoned to death![16]

There is no need to give weight to the ideas of people whose sole purpose is to find *any excuse* to reject Christ and *remain their own god* dedicated to the pursuit of self-pleasure.[17] They reject Jesus because the logos reality of Jesus *would require them to change*. To protect their lifestyle, they will remain quarrelsome[18] and hard-hearted, resisting anything of God[19] until they realize the hole in their life can only be filled by Christ when they accept His authority and His gift (*Himself!*). *Pause and digest — agree, disagree, or discuss?*

God's Word Is Universal

Since the Bible is the 'word of God', is every single English word critical? Some people get stuck on this, saying "See, it says right here, . . ." but then a different translation has a slightly different English word! Now what? It is good to keep in mind the English words are only

---

[14] John 17:17 "Sanctify them by the truth; Your word is truth."

[15] *More Than a Carpenter*, Josh McDowell, Ch. 5, "Bibliographical Test"

[16] Acts 7:59 "While they were stoning him, Stephen appealed, 'Lord Jesus, receive my spirit.'"

[17] 2 Timothy 3:2 "For men will be lovers of themselves, lovers of money, boastful, arrogant, abusive, disobedient to their parents, ungrateful, unholy, . . ."

[18] 2 Timothy 2:23 "But reject foolish and ignorant speculation, for you know that it breeds quarreling."

[19] Acts 7:51 "You stiff-necked and uncircumcised in heart and ears always resist the Holy Spirit; as your fathers did, also do you."

critical to correctly convey God's *ideas*, which is why there are many Bible translations and why this book refers many words to their original Greek.

Hear this: God *is greater than single words!* It is the fullness of God's *ideas* that are critical, they interlock perfectly with everything He says,[20] and they repeat.

This is key in your Trinity + You relationship. The 'words' of God, or 'logos', are not simply English letters on the page or 'mouth sounds'. Logos are *ideas* that impact, concepts that force change, and have meanings with consequences to test, trust, and have <u>relationship</u> with in our life.[21]

The original living Word (logos) is Jesus, part of God,[22] who became flesh so that we could experience the <u>true</u> nature of God[23] and *have relationship* with Him[24] through the Holy Spirit.

If the logos were just letters on a page, the Bible would simply be a dry self-help book with little impact. And for some it is! But for those with an absorbing *relationship* to Jesus, the Bible impacts our transformation since it is another way to understand the logos (ideas) that God wants us to try to know.

Therefore, the Bible is fine in any language[25] (including Hindi, Arabic, Korean, even Swahili!) because His *Word* transcends physical language and speaks to the spiritual heart of humanity (our need for love; God is the <u>only way</u> to fully satisfy that need).

It is *God's* logos message (love of us!) that enables Him to produce good fruit *in* our lives and *through* our lives. Good fruit (love) is not produced from arguing[26] over punctuation when translating 33 AD Greek to 2024 English (American, Australian, or Irish English!). Good fruit is produced by joining ourselves to Jesus. Therefore, any Bible

---

[20] Hebrews 13:8 "Jesus Christ is the same yesterday and today and forever."

[21] 2 Timothy 3:15 "From infancy you have known the Holy Scriptures, which are able to make you wise for salvation through faith in Christ Jesus."

[22] John 1:1 "In the beginning was the Word, and the Word was with God, and the Word was God."

[23] John 1:14 "The Word became flesh and made His dwelling among us. We have seen His glory, the glory of the one and only Son from the Father, full of grace and truth."

[24] John 1:12 "But to all who did receive Him, to those who believed in His name, He gave the right to become children of God . . ."

[25] Isaiah 55:11 ". . . so My word that proceeds from My mouth will not return to Me empty, but it will accomplish what I please, and it will prosper where I send it."

[26] Mark 9:34 "But they were silent, for on the way they had been arguing about which of them was the greatest."

translation, paraphrase, truncation (like a pocket Gideon given to soldiers that omits Job), or pastor's sermon *which makes you yearn and reach for a greater union with the real Jesus* is 'good'.[27] In fact, it is wise to use all the resources (Greek, commentaries, etc.) available to us to see how God's ideas (logos) interlock since it helps our reliance[28] in Him. As long as *this too* doesn't become a stressful do-do trap, let us not limit God helping *us* grow in *Him*!

To go from knowing *about* Jesus to *being one* with Jesus, we must immerse ourselves in His word, any and all of it, until we become more in-synch with Him as an expression of *His living Word*.[29] The more we are in-synch with Jesus, the more peace we will have loving without fear from the power[30] of His Holy Spirit flowing through us.

Logos, the Word, is at work transforming[31] you. The more we are absorbed in the living and fixed Word (Jesus and the Bible), the more we progress[32] in maturity. To be *most successful*, we must reach in the bowl and feed ourselves[33] — by tuning-in to Christ's love for us!

Absorbed in the Word

Immersing ourselves in the fixed word should be as *comfortable* as being with the living Word. Day and night[34] immersion can be done any way that works for you:

- Bible reading in line, on airplanes, in quiet times or loud.
- Bible *listening* in the car, replacing other audio we choose, or complimenting a lazy day.
- Memorize verses or *sing* them.[35]

---

[27] Jeremiah 15:16 "Your words were found, and I ate them. Your words became my joy and my heart's delight. For I bear Your name, O LORD God of Hosts."

[28] See Chapter 23 "Faith, Pistis 4102"

[29] 1 Corinthians 6:17 "But he who unites himself with the Lord is one with Him in spirit."

[30] Ephesians 6:10 "Finally, be strong in the Lord and in His mighty power."

[31] 1 Thessalonians 2:13 "And we continually thank God because, when you received the word of God that you heard from us, you accepted it not as the word of men, but as the true word of God—the word which is now at work in you who believe."

[32] 1 Timothy 4:15 "Ponder these things; be absorbed in them, so that your progress may be evident to all."

[33] Proverbs 26:15 "The slacker buries his hand in the dish; it wearies him to bring it back to his mouth."

[34] Joshua 1:8 "This Book of the Law must not depart from your mouth; meditate on it day and night, so that you may be careful to do everything written in it. For then you will prosper and succeed in all you do."

[35] Matthew 26:30 "And when they had sung a hymn, they went out to the Mount of

- Write a poem about a Bible idea (logos).[36]
- Put scriptures on your wall, door frame,[37] or electronic screen.
- Compare sections from different translations, the Greek online, or different books of the same event (Peter chops off an ear! John 18:3-11, Matthew 26:47-56, Mark 14:43-50, Luke 22:47-53).
- Research a scripture question through sermons or commentaries, "What's up with *that* verse?"
- Listen to music and challenge its message to biblical verses (how "sweet a sound" is "amazing grace"?), or just close your eyes and immerse yourself listening.
- Ask challenge questions to apply the *fixed* and *living* Word to current and future life (lab grown organs, pre-packaged food, home delivery, living on Mars — God aligned or not?).
- Ask *Him!* "God, how should I shape my life?"
- Do-do nothing! Rest in Jesus. His presence is THE most important thing. Know He loves you and simply enjoy it — "Thank you Jesus!"

Immersion in the fixed word can be as *dynamic* as the *living* Word — keep your relationship to it fresh. Enjoy it! Make it part of your life worship[38] (praise, thankfulness, enjoyment of His blessings, refreshment in God's creation, hymns, prayer, Godly striving, loving others). *Pause and digest — agree, disagree, or discuss?*

Christianity is a rare religion that <u>allows</u> testing[39] and still, the Bible passes all reasonable tests. There will always be some mysteries that remain,[40] since we are not God, nor are we in Heaven.

Olives."

[36] *The Sidewalk Ends at God* by Emmanuel DeWeg ISBN 9781640324060

[37] Deuteronomy 6:9 "Write them on the doorposts of your houses and on your gates."

[38] Colossians 3:16 "Let the word of Christ richly dwell within you as you teach and admonish one another with all wisdom, and as you sing psalms, hymns, and spiritual songs with gratitude in your hearts to God."

[39] James 1:3 ". . . knowing that testing of your faith produces endurance."

[40] 1 Timothy 3:16 "By common confession, the mystery of godliness is great: He appeared in the flesh, was vindicated by the Spirit, was seen by angels, was proclaimed among the nations, was believed in throughout the world, was taken up in glory."

We have everything we need in every translation to live as a new, amazing, creation of God:[41] God loves you and wants a relationship with you through Jesus Christ (not do-do performance).[42]

These are such simple ideas,[43] logos, words, but when we know them, feel them, ache for them, and live them, God's love and relationship <u>transforms</u> our lives and the lives of those around us.[44]

You are God's tiny mustard seed of love, growing into a mighty tree spreading love across your branches.[45]

You are God's little leaven of love, that is spreading love across the whole dough.[46]

These are the words, logos, ideas, meanings and significance of the Trinity + You relationship.

What Word of God will you *let move you* today, right now?[47]

What Does This All Mean?

—Being in-synch with the living Word, Jesus, leads to being
 —Transformed by the living Word, which leads to
  —Radiating the living Word.

---

[41] Isaiah 43:19 "Behold, I am about to do something new; even now it is coming. Do you not see it? Indeed, I will make a way in the wilderness and streams in the desert."

[42] Hebrews 12:17 "For you know that afterward, when he wanted to inherit the blessing, he was rejected. He could find no ground for repentance, though he sought the blessing with tears."

[43] 1 Corinthians 1:21 "For since in the wisdom of God the world through its wisdom did not know Him, God was pleased through the foolishness of what was preached to save those who believe."

[44] 2 Corinthians 3:18 "And we, who with unveiled faces all reflect the glory of the Lord, are being transformed into His image with intensifying glory, which comes from the Lord, who is the Spirit."

[45] Luke 13:19 "It is like a mustard seed that a man tossed into his garden. It grew and became a tree, and the birds of the air nested in its branches."

[46] Luke 13:21 "It is like leaven that a woman took and mixed into three measures of flour, until all of it was leavened."

[47] Psalm 119:105 "Your word is a lamp to my feet and a light to my path."

19. Another, Allélón, 240

The Bible says, "Love one another."[1] How do we actually <u>do</u> this!?[2] Does that mean <u>everybody</u>? In all the same way? Even those that take advantage of us? Isn't loving God enough?

What does the Bible mean when it says "another"?

▲ Certain People   ▲ Everybody

The answer is. . . it depends on the context — so watch Bible verses carefully! And know you can always <u>ask Him</u> how to live *this moment* in His Love.

Definitions and Demarks

To understand "another" we need to revisit the Bible definitions and be clear on "love", as there are different *kinds* of love and different love *actions* for different people. "Love" (agapé based) has three variations in the Bible (a Trinity of Love?):

Greek	'Love' English Definition	Impact
agapéto 27	*adjective:* 'beloved'	**You are 'loved' by Jesus Christ, and because you are loved this . . .**
agapé 26	*noun:* your 'state of being', or desire of goodwill and charity	**makes you into love,[3] which leads to . . .**
agapaó 25	*verb:* action of love; your desire causes actions and intent[4]	**you loving another.**

---

[1] John 13:34 "A new commandment I give you: Love one another. As I have loved you, so you also must love one another."

[2] Romans 7:18 "I know that nothing good lives in me, that is, in my flesh; for I have the desire to do what is good, but I cannot carry it out."

[3] 1 John 4:19 "We love because He first loved us."

[4] 1 John 4:12 "No one has ever seen God; but if we love one another, God remains

Christ *loving us* leads to our 'love' *state of being* and *actions* to others. Our do-do actions *do not* make us love more as Christians, *only* the love flowing through us from Jesus Christ does.

Or as a formula:

Jesus → Love Relationship → Us → Love Relationship → Others

If "God *is love*", and we are 'in' God, then we "*is love*" only when we are 'in' God.[5] When we take our eyes off of Jesus, what are we then? Atheists going to Heaven? Sheep running off? Prodigal children? No need to focus on the label. Simply focus on being in-tune with God! Let not our pride, the Liar, or our flesh distract us from Jesus Christ. *Pause and digest — agree, disagree, or discuss?*

To Everybody — Love State

We can be a light in this world[6] — to everybody. Just as God sends the rain down on everyone, we can be goodwill as *He* is goodwill.[7] We can be merciful since *He* is merciful.[8] We can forgive, since *He* forgave us.[9]

These attitudes, desires, and intent, is a *state of being*. To everybody, we can exist in *God's* 'love state of being' (agapé) without going crazy that we are not do-do-doing enough. We can do acts of goodwill as needs arise. We do not wish harm for another ("as yourself"). We hope others bow their hearts to Christ ("as yourself"). But we're also not going door to door shoving tracts and cookies into everyone's hands.

This 'love state of being' of goodwill and charity can only come from the love of Jesus. You do not get this love from 'trying' or 'working harder' since 'trying' is just your own do-do without Jesus. If we could do it ourselves, we wouldn't need Jesus!

---

in us, and His love is perfected in us."

[5] Isaiah 26:3 "You will keep in perfect peace the steadfast of mind, because he trusts in You."

[6] Acts 13:47 "For this is what the Lord has commanded us: 'I have made you a light for the Gentiles, to bring salvation to the ends of the earth.'"

[7] Matthew 5:45 "... that you may be sons of your Father in heaven. He causes His sun to rise on the evil and the good, and sends rain on the righteous and the unrighteous."

[8] Luke 6:36 "Be merciful, just as your Father is merciful."

[9] Colossians 3:13 "Bear with one another and forgive any complaint you may have against someone else. Forgive as the Lord forgave you."

To Everybody — Love Action

Since God helps us be in a love 'state of being' (agapé) to everybody, then it makes sense we should have some love 'action' (agapaó) for everybody as well — even strangers.[10] Express to everybody *actions* of goodwill, charity, kindness, patience, and mercy[11] as you are able and as makes sense *in the moment*.

Beyond a single love 'action' in the moment, multiple and frequent long-term love 'actions' create relationships. In healthy relationships we need to understand the healthy boundaries of the relationship. For healthy relationships, love 'action' as you *and they* are able and produces good fruit, without demanding more. Hope and work for better relationships — yes. *Demand* more relationship? No. (can one even 'demand' a relationship?)

Another; ἀλλήλων; allélón:
Strong's 240. One another, themselves, or the parties of the relationship. Could have obligations attached, but may not.

We live in a world of boo-boos and scars that are hard to overcome, making all relationships rocky until we get to Heaven. Live faithfully[12] in-tune with Jesus and the Holy Spirit to see where good relationship boundaries lie and that truth will set you free from the chains[13] of expectation.

To Believers — Love Action

Now for certain "others", specifically believers,[14] the Bible details additional ways to fulfill "Love one another" actions. Of course it does! One can only fellowship[15] in spiritual ways to those *who have the Holy Spirit!*

---

[10] Hebrews 13:2 "Do not neglect to show hospitality to strangers, for by so doing some people have entertained angels without knowing it."

[11] 1 Peter 4:8 "Above all, love one another deeply, because love covers over a multitude of sins."

[12] 3 John 1:4 "I have no greater joy than to hear that my children are walking in the truth."

[13] Jeremiah 40:4 "But now, behold, I am freeing you today from the chains that were on your wrists."

[14] Matthew 12:50 "For whoever does the will of My Father in heaven is My brother and sister and mother."

[15] 1 John 1:7 "But if we walk in the light as He is in the light, we have fellowship with one another, and the blood of Jesus His Son cleanses us from all sin."

Peter clearly shows these different love 'actions' to different people groups when he said to *honor* all people but *love* the brotherhood.[16]

Watch the Word carefully for special love actions by and to believers:

- For correction,[17] encouragement,[18] and guidance.[19]
- For duties based on roles.[20]
- For extra support[21] or rewards.[22]

Pause and digest — agree, disagree, or discuss?

Practice

When it comes to love in all three forms, *practice makes perfect!*[23] The more we *practice* the Trinity + You love in both *state of being* and *action (outpouring God's love to others)*, the stronger is our spiritual growth in the Trinity + You relationship.[24] Loving God alone is not enough. To grow, we *must* love others. Such spiritual growth lets even non-believers know that you are a disciple of Christ.[25]

How To Practice

"Love one another" requires two free-choice parties to relate to each other, but *how* they relate is as dynamic as the participants. There are no fixed rules. God therefore gives us brains to use discretion.[26] Are you using it to know how to act and when not to?

---

[16] 1 Peter 2:17 "Treat everyone with high regard: Love the brotherhood of believers, fear God, honor the king."

[17] Galatians 6:1 "Brothers, if someone is caught in a trespass, you who are spiritual should restore him with a spirit of gentleness. But watch yourself, or you also may be tempted."

[18] Romans 1:12 "... that is, that you and I may be mutually encouraged by each other's faith."

[19] Colossians 3:22 "Slaves, obey your earthly masters in everything, not only to please them while they are watching, but with sincerity of heart and fear of the Lord."

[20] Ephesians 5:25 "Husbands, love your wives, just as Christ loved the church and gave Himself up for her, ..."

[21] Romans 16:1 "I commend to you our sister Phoebe, a servant of the church in Cenchrea."

[22] Mark 4:25 "For whoever has will be given more. But whoever does not have, even what he has will be taken away from him."

[23] 1 John 2:5 "But whoever may keep His word, truly in him the love of God has been perfected. By this we know that we are in Him."

[24] James 2:24 "As you can see, a man is justified by his deeds and not by faith alone."

[25] John 13:35 "By this everyone will know that you are My disciples, if you love one another."

[26] Proverbs 1:4 "To impart prudence to the simple and knowledge and discretion to

When answering "how to act", did you answer *all* yourself? If so, you just took your eyes off Jesus! Remember to include the *Holy Spirit* on what to do and confirm it in the Bible! Ask for *His* discretion. It's no longer just you; it is the Trinity + You!

Old habits, like leaning on our own understanding,[27] need to be replaced with the spiritual wisdom available from Jesus Christ. Your heart may be trying to align with God's aims, but this decision-making process needs *His spiritual* checks between your thought and action.[28] *Pause and digest — agree, disagree, or discuss?*

Tune-In; See from God

Just as we tune-in our spiritual relationship with God, we can tune-in to others to have better relationships with them. Ask yourself, "How does God see?" If we try to see others *and ourselves* with the eyes of God, it can redefine *everything* in a compassionate, loving way.

God sees a person's life from beginning to end — so too can we be compassionate about that (did they grow up sick or poor or rejected?). God sees the person's spirit (heart) and mood (feelings) and isn't shocked about the person's physical appearance or noise they make — so can we. We can bring all of this spiritual view to understand as we relate to another person *in this moment*.

- Are we seeking to understand others, or do *we want* to be understood?
- Are we listening to others, or focused on what *we want* to say?
- Do we care about others' careers, acclaim, and comfort, or do *we want* the focus on ourselves?

Liberate Love; Drop the Judgements

Leaving judgement to God breaks down our barriers to tuning-in to others. It is easy to judge others when we don't understand others the way that God does. When we try to see *with* God, we mature with the compassion and charity *of* God.

---

the young, . . ."

[27] Proverbs 28:26 "He who trusts in himself is a fool, but one who walks in wisdom will be safe."

[28] James 5:8 "You also be patient; strengthen your hearts, because the coming of the Lord has drawn near."

Who are we to judge:[29]
- The poor person whose whole life is about surviving day-to-day from the day they were born?
- The old man angry at God from the day he lost his wife?
- Yourself(!) as you overcome your past and its effects in your life today.

Reality

Though we shouldn't *judge* others with human eyes, and can better understand others by living through the Trinity + You union, it does *not* mean we need to expose ourselves to the bad fruit and or danger of "another".[30]

Discretion

Spiritual discretion is the *key* to methods and boundaries that produce the most good fruit of Jesus Christ in ourselves, our relationships, and in others, without the living water getting "choked off".[31]

Ask the Holy Spirit to open our eyes to His *specific* guidance about *general* things:
- That we don't become evil combating evil.[32]
- That our burden should not be for others' ease.[33]
- That we feed the *actually* hungry and *actually* thirsty, not the want-y that put their hands out.[34]
- That we don't become enablers; that "others" are participating in their own success when they can.[35]

---

[29] James 4:11 "Do not speak against one another, brothers. The one speaking against his brother or judging his brother speaks against the Law and judges the Law. But if you judge the Law, you are not a doer of the Law, but a judge."

[30] 2 John 1:11 "Whoever greets such a person shares in his evil deeds."

[31] Matthew 13:7 "And other fell upon the thorns, and the thorns grew up and choked them."

[32] 1 Peter 3:9 "Do not repay evil with evil or insult with insult, but with blessing, because to this you were called so that you may inherit a blessing."

[33] 2 Corinthians 8:13 "It is not our intention that others may be relieved while you are burdened, but that there may be equality."

[34] Romans 12:20 "On the contrary, 'If your enemy is hungry, feed him; if he is thirsty, give him a drink. For in so doing, you will heap burning coals on his head.'"

[35] 2 Thessalonians 3:10 "For even while we were with you, we gave you this command: 'If anyone is unwilling to work, he shall not eat.'"

Also ask the Holy Spirit for His *general* guidance about *specific* things:

- When to go[36] and when to stay.[37]
- When to be peaceable, and when to shake the dust off your feet.[38]
- When to be hospitable, and when you shouldn't even greet others.[39]
- When to let the relationship grow, and when to cut it off.[40]

Seeing and living life through the Trinity + You union shows who we,[41] and others, truly are *and should be* in the spirit, that enables us to have the most fruitful relationship possible in that moment, that place, with that person. *Pause and digest — agree, disagree, or discuss?*

Not Now

There will be times, seasons, or even lifetimes, when some people, for whatever the reason, will *not* be able to relate to you in goodwill, nor produce any good fruit relating with you.

Likewise, there are times and places and people where *you* will not be able to relate in goodwill, because of your history, how the other person is communicating and triggering you, or maybe because in this moment you don't have goodwill for yourself (you can't have goodwill for a neighbor if you don't have goodwill for yourself).[42]

Accept this, and ask the Holy Spirit (our Helper!)[43] to keep the relationship to a level and method that makes as much good fruit as you

---

[36] Acts 12:9 "So Peter followed him out, but he was unaware that what the angel was doing was real. He thought he was only seeing a vision."

[37] Acts 16:28 "But Paul called out in a loud voice, 'Do not harm yourself! We are all here!'"

[38] Matthew 10:14 "And if anyone will not welcome you or heed your words, shake the dust off your feet when you leave that home or town."

[39] 2 John 1:10 "If anyone comes to you but does not bring this teaching, do not receive him into your home or even greet him."

[40] 2 Timothy 3:5 ". . . having a form of godliness but denying its power. Turn away from such as these!"

[41] Jude 1:21 "Keep yourselves in the love of God as you await the mercy of our Lord Jesus Christ to bring you eternal life."

[42] Romans 13:9 ". . . other commandments, are summed up in this one decree: 'Love your neighbor as yourself.'"

[43] John 14:16 "And I will ask the Father, and He will give you another Helper, that He may be with you to the age."

and they can, which may include none at all. *Pause and digest — agree, disagree, or discuss?*

God Transforms

Always reach out to the Holy Spirit for guidance. It can make the relationship and or the *understanding of the relationship* better, both in the moment and long term. It may be as simple a prayer as this, "Lord help me!"[44]

God defines what is 'good'.[45] Utilizing the wisdom available to us in the Trinity + You union will help your relationships become healthier. God knows best (though the world disagrees!).

And God knows *everything*. He knows every good and horrible thing that you and the "other" has been through and *will* go through. Our best path to transform our relationship to "others" is to cling to Jesus. What seems impossible in the physical realm *becomes possible*[46] when we live in the spiritual realm hand in hand with Jesus.

How? In Christ.

How do we actually, "Love one another"? Really, how do we *do* this? You can't plan for it, organize it, or 'committee' it. Love has to come from the Trinity, through You, to "another", right now, in this moment. Not an hour ago, nor an hour from now, nor being placed into a schedule — *now*. Relating *now*, in *this moment*, is all the opportunity we have to love, just as God loves us.[47]

God is Love,
Submit to *His* love, so that
You can "love one another"
as you and they are able, *as He guides.*

Should you test this message? Always![48] How? Try it today. Ask God from your heart what you need. Or ask this to get you started:

---

[44] Matthew 15:25 "The woman came and knelt before Him. 'Lord, help me!' she said."

[45] James 1:17 "Every good and perfect gift is from above, coming down from the Father of the heavenly lights, with whom there is no change or shifting shadow."

[46] Luke 18:27 "But He said, 'The things impossible with men are possible with God.'"

[47] 1 John 4:11 "Beloved, if God so loved us, we also ought to love one another."

[48] Revelation 2:2 "I know your deeds, your labor, and your perseverance. I know that you cannot tolerate those who are evil, and you have tested and exposed as liars those who falsely claim to be apostles."

"Lord, I submit to your love. Help me know how much you love me. Let me hear your voice stronger than ever. Help me see others as you see them. Guide me how to love others today. Help me when I feel unable. Give me your power to love without fear. In Jesus's name I pray. Amen."

20. Fruit, Karpos 2590

Since your physical body will not go to Heaven, how should we live here on earth?[1] In a life without The Law, how do we <u>know</u> we are doing a good job? How do we <u>know</u> what we are consuming is good? What does a 'Christian' even look like? Does God care what we produce in our physical life? If so, how do we produce more? What is all this talk about 'fruit'?

What does 'fruit' mean?

▲ Weirdo ▲ Results

High Level

'Fruit' is the shorthand description to show what you are producing with or without God, good or bad.[2] It represents the *physical* world of, 'look-there-it-is,' as well Christ's *spiritual* transformation of us.[3] Interestingly, when we see 'good fruit' in the Bible, it often means *both* the *spiritual* transformation and the *physical* evidence this spiritual transformation produces in our life.

'Good fruit' is defined by God.[4] God placed the ultimate example of 'good fruit' — Jesus — in the womb of man[5] as the seed *for everyone* to produce 'good fruit'.[6] Today Jesus produces His fruit *through us* in the Trinity + You relationship *if we ask or tune-in to His will.*[7] Pause and digest — agree, disagree, or discuss?

---

[1] 2 Peter 3:11 "Since everything will be destroyed in this way, what kind of people ought you to be? You ought to conduct yourselves in holiness and godliness. . ."

[2] James 3:18 "And the fruit of righteousness is sown in peace by those making peace."

[3] Matthew 3:8 "Produce fruit, then, in keeping with [a new mind (metanoeó 3340)]".

[4] Galatians 5:22 "But the fruit of the Spirit is love, joy, peace, patience, kindness, <u>goodness</u>, faithfulness, . . ."

[5] Luke 1:42 ". . . and she cried out in a loud voice and said, 'Blessed are you among women, and blessed is the fruit your of womb.'"

[6] John 12:24 "Truly, truly, I tell you, unless a kernel of wheat falls to the ground and dies, it remains only a seed; but if it dies, it bears much fruit."

[7] John 15:16 "You did not choose Me, but I chose you. And I appointed you to go and bear fruit—fruit that will remain—so that whatever you ask the Father in My name, He will give you."

Good Fruit Test

What does it mean to ask if 'this is good fruit'?

If we ask this about ourselves, our 'fruit' is a test of *us*, evidenced by our worldly bad and God's good.[8] Looking at our 'fruit' guides us to know when we are living in-tune spiritually and physically in Jesus by the *fruit we produce*,[9] and therefore helps us get back in-tune *with Him*.

'Fruit' is also a test of the inputs to our lives. TV shows, preachers, the 'news', 'wisdom' on the internet, there are plenty of wolves dressed in white[10] trying to influence us or running Bible schools for the Liar.[11]

Should you even be reading *this book (The Do-Do Trap)* without testing it against God's word? Heavens no! Thankfully there *are* plenty of great resources to help us learn and strengthen our relationship to God — but test them for their fruits![12] *Pause and digest — agree, disagree, or discuss?*

Through the Trinity + You

Trying to produce 'good fruit' without God will be *dry fruit*. It will be a shadow of the bounty available through the Trinity + You union. The Living Water — Jesus — is what makes each of us juicy![13]

Our job is to learn and practice *being* juicy through *Him*:

- <u>Choose</u> to live in the Trinity + You guidance moment by moment, as His guidance works for all times.[14]
- <u>Fill</u> yourself in His knowledge (The Word, Jesus)[15]

---

[8] Romans 6:22 "But now, having been set free from sin, and having become slaves to God, you have your fruit unto sanctification, and the end *is* eternal life."

[9] Matthew 12:33 "Make a tree good and its fruit will be good, or make a tree bad and its fruit will be bad; for a tree is known by its fruit."

[10] Matthew 7:16 "By their fruit you will recognize them. Are grapes gathered from thornbushes, or figs from thistles?"

[11] Revelation 3:9 "Look at those who belong to the synagogue of Satan, who claim to be [my followers] but are liars instead. I will make them come and bow down at your feet, and they will know that I love you."

[12] Ephesians 5:10 "Test and prove what pleases the Lord."

[13] 1 Corinthians 12:7 "Now to each one the manifestation of the Spirit is given for the common good."

[14] 1 John 2:17 "The world is passing away, along with its desires; but whoever does the will of God remains forever."

[15] Philippians 1:11 ". . . filled with the fruit of righteousness that comes through Jesus Christ, to the glory and praise of God."

- *Practice* letting the Living Water flow through you to produce His fruit,[16] as His branch instead of trying to be the source root.

Results

Letting Jesus be our source and guide is very liberating since the branch can't do anything without the vine.[17] It is not on *your* shoulders to create God's kingdom through your own do-do works. It is up to God *through* you *if you let Him*, to create it and rejoice together.[18]

> **Fruit; καρπός; karpos:**
> Strong's 2590. Used 66 times. Literally, the crop we eat. Figuratively, the results.

Practicing living through Jesus allows you to *understand* and *be* His truth, His love, and His life — His fruit! His *eternal fruit!*[19] Learn to *accept your love from God* and you will *learn how to love others*. Accepting 'love' from Him, which will overflow to others, is more important than all our do-do "sacrifices".[20] Our self-created do-do works may look like a bounty on earth but count for nothing in Heaven.[21]

It is not *what* you do that is important. It is *how* you do it that is important. Are you do-do-doing 'good deeds' *your* way, or are you listening to Jesus's guidance? By living in the Trinity + You union *spiritually* to act in life *physically*, you won't be spending your own energy and the fruit produced will multiply 30, 60, or 100 times (Jesus said so!).[22] *Pause and digest — agree, disagree, or discuss?*

---

[16] John 15:2 "He cuts off every branch in Me that bears no fruit, and every branch that does bear fruit, He prunes to make it even more fruitful."

[17] John 15:4 "Remain in Me, and I will remain in you. Just as no branch can bear fruit by itself unless it remains in the vine, neither can you bear fruit unless you remain in Me."

[18] John 4:36 "The *one* reaping receives a reward and gathers fruit unto eternal life, so that the *one* sowing and the *one* reaping may rejoice together."

[19] Matthew 6:20 "But store up for yourselves treasures in heaven, where moth and rust do not destroy, and where thieves do not break in and steal."

[20] Mark 12:33 "... and to love Him with all your heart and with all your understanding and with all your strength, and to love your neighbor as yourself, which is more important than all burnt offerings and sacrifices."

[21] Luke 12:17 "And he was reasoning within himself, saying, 'What shall I do, for I have nowhere I will store up my fruits?'"

[22] Matthew 13:8 "Still other seed fell on good soil and produced a crop—a hundredfold, sixtyfold, or thirtyfold."

Submit Your Heart

Do-do-doing things 'our way' can spoil God's fruit and plans. Just because it is 'good' doesn't mean it is *God's* 'good'. After all these years, we humans can still decide to act on our own, just like Adam and Eve![23] 'Our way' is plastic fruit, that seems good but has no juice, no God, and therefore hollow of love — *God* is the filler of love![24] Instead, let us *continually* offer to God our heart through the Trinity + You relationship, which by its structure is submitting to God, listening and acting in accordance to the one that really knows best — God![25]

When we become a Christian, by default we continue to lead our own life. We know no better. This is like being asked by God to dance, and then insisting that we lead all the steps! But we *can* know better.

Ask the Holy Spirit to lead us, show us, help us, and then *listen and act* to His urgings flowing through our hearts. The Holy Spirit is *always* inside of you, ready to be asked![26] The Holy Spirit is part of the Trinity *designed* by God and Jesus to join with you, guiding you to *their* will, which is *love*.

It is in God's season that we are fruitful.[27] It is Jesus that provides us patience[28] for the trees to grow, the flower to bloom, the rains to come, the fruit to set, and finally to harvest the 'good fruit' as the He determines best.[29]

How do we be *more* fruitful? How do we make sure our fruit drips with the Living Water of Love?

---

[23] Genesis 3:6 "So when the woman saw that the tree was good for food, and that it was a delight to the eyes, and that the tree was to be desired to make one wise, she took of its fruit and ate, and she also gave some to her husband who was with her, and he ate."

[24] 1 Corinthians 13:3 "If I give all I possess to the poor and exult in the surrender of my body, but have not love, I gain nothing."

[25] Hebrews 13:15 "Through Jesus, therefore, let us continually offer to God a sacrifice of praise, the fruit of lips that confess His name."

[26] Romans 8:9 "You, however, are controlled not by the flesh, but by the Spirit, if the Spirit of God lives in you. And if anyone does not have the Spirit of Christ, he does not belong to Christ."

[27] Acts 14:17 "Yet He has not left Himself without testimony to His goodness: He gives you rain from heaven and fruitful seasons, filling your hearts with food and gladness."

[28] James 5:7 "Be patient, then, brothers, until the Lord's coming. See how the farmer awaits the precious fruit of the soil — how patient he is for the fall and spring rains."

[29] Mark 4:29 "And when the fruit offers itself, he sends the sickle immediately, for the harvest has come."

Pick This Fruit

The Spirit of God produces His Fruit: love, joy, peace, patience, kindness, goodness, faithfulness, gentleness, self-control.

Submit to *His* Spirit, so that
You live by His Spirit, and walk by His Spirit,
Sharing His Fruit with others
as you and they are able
as He is fruitful in you.

21. Pray, Proseuchomai 4336

Why pray? Why pray for safety if you can still get in a car accident? What went wrong? What if you pray for a healing and the person graduates to Heaven, is that, "all things for good"?[1] Heavens no! Does God not care or did you not have enough 'faith' or is God punishing you when you skipped 'morning prayer time in the closet'? Of course not! God is LOVE! So then, what do we do with all these weird things we hear about prayer?

What is 'prayer'?

▲	▲	▲
Something we're told to do, like flossing.	The most important religious thing, though we don't get how, or why.	What you do to begin eating.

High Level

To really understand prayer, we must *expand our definition* of prayer. Prayer is not limited to 'us talking to God'. Prayer is an *exchange of our mindset with the Trinity's* (God, Jesus, and the Holy Spirit). The Greek word for 'pray' (proseuchomai) is a literal joining of the words 'exchange desire' (pros = exchange [4314] and euchomai = desire or wish [2172]). *Prayer transforms our mind's desires.[2]*

'Mindset desire exchange' is the deeper definition of 'prayer' *in practice*, the *method* of God's promise to give us a new mind (metanoeó

---

[1] A good example for looking at verses broadly and specifically. Broadly, Romans 8 is about spiritual love, spiritual things, and the spiritual Trinity + You relationship. Specifically, looking at the Greek, an alternate relationship-based reading of Romans 8:28 "... in all things God [cooperates (sunergeó 4903)] for the good of those who love Him, ..." instead of "all things [cooperate (sunergeó 4903)] for good to those who love God..." There is much discussion about this verse online, but for this author (who can be wrong), the relationship-based reading aligns more with the rest of the Bible of God working *in us* through His Holy Spirit regardless of the circumstances.

[2] Romans 12:2 "And do not be conformed to this age, but be transformed by the renewing of the mind, for you to prove what is the good and well-pleasing and perfect will of God."

3340).³ Prayer brings our yearnings, thanks, concerns, and fears to God, and God responds (in words, peace, emotion, insight, urgings, out of ordinary happenings, etc.) for us to accept or reject as free-choice beings. *Pause and digest — agree, disagree, or discuss?*

Prayer is *spiritual* exchange, as dynamic and living as the Trinity + You relationship, which may be why many lack vibrancy in Christ. It is easier and more comfortable to follow a checklist of do-do actions than participate in a real, living, fulfilling prayer relationship with Jesus Christ.

To have a relationship with Jesus, we need:
1. a heart that *yearns* to partake in the union
2. a soul that takes *action* to pursue that relationship
3. the strength to *let go* of control and submit to Jesus⁴

Prayer provides the *method* to have this relationship, a <u>way</u> to have our mindsets exchanged in the Trinity + You union. Prayer is <u>how</u> our thought, mood, and spirit is <u>shared</u> with the Trinity, and the prayer process includes the Trinity's <u>response</u> if we are open to it!

The Bible is *not* the vehicle for a relationship with Jesus. The Bible can't be a living relationship vehicle since the Bible is *fixed*. The Bible is informational, guiding, and great for testing what we think is an answer to our prayer. *Living relationships* need a method with *living* interactions, moment by moment mindset exchanges, exchanges that happen automatically when we pray and open ourselves to Jesus's response. *Pause and digest — agree, disagree, or discuss?*

How, When, and Where to Pray

With the Holy Spirit inside you, by Jesus conquering death⁵ so you can live with Him, and God wanting your relationship for eternity,⁶ do you think it matters how you hold your hands when you pray? *Pause and digest — agree, disagree, or discuss?*

---

³ 2 Timothy 2:25 "He must gently reprove those who oppose him, in the hope that God may grant them [a new mind (metanoeó 3340)] leading to a knowledge of the truth."

⁴ Deuteronomy 6:5 "And you shall love the LORD your God with all your heart and with all your soul and with all your strength."

⁵ John 11:25 "Jesus said to her, 'I am the resurrection and the life. Whoever believes in Me will live, even though he dies.'"

⁶ Colossians 1:22 "But now He has reconciled you by Christ's physical body through death to present you holy, unblemished, and blameless in His presence . . ."

If praying is the method for mindset exchange in the Trinity + You relationship, how much does it matter if we pray 'head-down-kneeling' or 'hands-up-standing'?[7] Does God restrict our relationship to praying 'predawn-closet-hiding-King-James-language'?[8] Of course not! God is not limited by do-do rules![9]

All this *physical* stuff doesn't matter! What does matter is you spiritually yearning to communicate any way you can *continuously*.[10] Whether you are on the roof[11] or the mountain,[12] pray! *Pause and digest — agree, disagree, or discuss?*

Therefore, what are the best times, places or methods to exchange your yearnings with Jesus's yearnings? Continuously! Sing,[13] dance,[14] talk, groan,[15] scrapbook, vacuum[16] — let go of the do-do restrictions and be free in Christ to freely radiate *Christ*. If your spirit is yearning *He will*[17] relate with you as you are able.

Pray; προσεύχομαι; proseuchomai:
Strong's 4336. Used 86 times. Basic usage is speaking to God in all forms; asks, thanks, and praise. Deeper, an exchange of desires.

Has this *expanded* the definition of prayer more than it should? Or, has this definition *limited* the power of Jesus? *Pause and digest — agree, disagree, or discuss?*

---

[7] 1 Timothy 2:8 "Therefore I want the men everywhere to pray, lifting up holy hands, without anger or dissension."

[8] Matthew 6:6 "But when you pray, go into your room and shut the door and pray to your Father who is in secret. And your Father who sees in secret will reward you."

[9] Job 42:2 "I know that You can do all things and that no plan of Yours can be thwarted."

[10] Ephesians 6:18 "Pray in the Spirit at all times, with every kind of prayer and petition. To this end, stay alert with all perseverance in your prayers for all the saints."

[11] Acts 10:9 "The next day at about the sixth hour, as the men were approaching the city on their journey, Peter went up on the roof to pray."

[12] Luke 6:12 "In those days Jesus went out to the mountain to pray, and He spent the night in prayer to God."

[13] 1 Corinthians 14:15 "What then shall I do? I will pray with my spirit, but I will also pray with my mind. I will sing with my spirit, but I will also sing with my mind."

[14] 2 Samuel 6:14 "And David, wearing a linen ephod, danced with all his might before the LORD."

[15] Romans 8:26 "In the same way, the Spirit helps us in our weakness. For we do not know how we ought to pray, but the Spirit Himself intercedes for us with groans too deep for words."

[16] Ephesians 6:5 "Slaves, obey your earthly masters with respect and fear and sincerity of heart, just as you would obey Christ."

[17] Jeremiah 29:12 "Then you will call upon Me and come and pray to Me, and I will listen to you."

What to Pray

Exchanging our mindset with the Trinity's mindset means opening our spirit to the fullness,[18] glory and majesty of God.[19] Our praying to Him inherently acknowledges His attributes and His position as leader in our life. We are then free to share our mindset in exchange for His.

What are some things to pray?

1. Thanks and praise:[20]
 — of God's gifts; physical and spiritual[21]
 — of God's supremacy

2. Asks for help; ourselves and others:
 — wisdom and understanding[22]
 — how to love others[23]
 — physical aid (strength, healing, and good fruit)[24]
 — spiritual aid (strength, healing, and good fruit)[25]

3. How about just regular conversations with God for no good reason?

Really, pray for anything since He wants to relate to us. And then watch and listen![26] Keep your spiritual eyes and heart open for God's response. Your prayers *are* heard and God *is* responding, though usually not as we expect. We must be open to receive *what is* given back if there

---

[18] John 1:16 "From His fullness we have all received grace upon grace."

[19] Jude 1:25 "... to the only God our Savior be glory, majesty, dominion, and authority through Jesus Christ our Lord before all time, and now, and for all eternity. Amen."

[20] Psalm 32:11 "Be glad in the LORD and rejoice, O righteous ones; shout for joy, all you upright in heart."

[21] Did you enjoy breathing today? Give thanks!

[22] Proverbs 4:5 "Get wisdom, get understanding; do not forget my words or turn from them."

[23] Galatians 5:1 "For you, brothers, were called to freedom; but do not use your freedom as an opportunity for the flesh. Rather, serve one another in love."

[24] James 5:14 "Is any one of you sick? He should call the elders of the church to pray over him and anoint him with oil in the name of the Lord."

[25] 3 John 1:2 "Beloved, I pray that in every way you may prosper and enjoy good health, as your soul also prospers."

[26] Proverbs 4:10 "Listen, my son, and receive my words, and the years of your life will be many."

is to be an *honest* exchange, a change of our mindset (metanoeó 3340) with Jesus. *Pause and digest — agree, disagree, or discuss?*

Can one blab a monologue all day and expect there to be a mindset exchange? Of course not. We must watch, listen, and *receive*. The Trinity + You relationship strengthens from us becoming more in Christ, in union with Christ, and that means receiving the Living Water from Christ as it *comes* instead of trying to dictate when, where, and how the Living Water should flow.

Prayers Not Our Way

Joining Christ transforms your life. He doesn't promise us a life with no physical bumps, sadness, or hurt.[27] He *does* promise to be with us *through* it all,[28] inside of us.[29] Inside our *physical* being? No. He is part of our *spiritual* being (like love and peace). With this in mind, our *physical* purpose on earth becomes learning how to be *spiritually loved* by God, to radiate *His love to others*.

What about prayers that do not go as we asked? Did God not hear us? Of course He hears us![30] Did we ask amiss?[31] What is amiss is our *expectation of a specific response*. This is why 'prayer' need be viewed as a <u>mindset</u> exchange (my thoughts for His) instead of an <u>action</u> exchange (I do so He does). *Pause and digest — agree, disagree, or discuss?*

If we pray for safe travels but get into a car accident, did God 'fail' us? The answer depends on *how* our mindset is joined to His. He may have failed our *expectations* of a specific response, even while He *succeeds* in *love,* acting in love in a *physical* world of free-choice beings.

Our attention on the physical world instead of the spiritual world is another form of the "Problem of Pain"[32] (Why does God allow physical evil, pain, and death?). God can help the *temporary* — the physical you — but He is concerned about something greater — the *eternal* you —

---

[27] 2 Corinthians 11:24 "Five times I received from the Jews the forty lashes minus one."

[28] Matthew 28:20 "And surely I am with you always, even to the end of the age."

[29] 1 John 4:4 "You are of God, little children, and have overcome them, because the *One* in you is greater than the *one* in the world."

[30] Psalm 34:17 "The righteous cry out, and the LORD hears; He delivers them from all their troubles."

[31] James 4:3 "You ask and do not receive, because you ask wrongly, that you may spend it in your pleasures."

[32] This is the title and subject of a C. S. Lewis classic book. (This footnote fulfills the requirement that all Christian books reference C. S. Lewis.)

your spiritual heart.[33] He can heal disease but it is *your heart* that matters *most*. He wants us to mature (teleios 5046) by growing a loving, healed, heart. Our physical body decays (boy does it ever!), but our spirit will live forever.

Examples

We will never fully know why God doesn't make our lives free of distressful things when we pray for them to be removed,[34] but we can reason out some different perspectives analyzing the above car accident example.

Why you got into a car accident after praying for 'safe travels':

1. Prayer *was* answered — You *are* safe! Sure, your car is totaled, but did you give thanks for being *alive*?
2. Free-choice — From 0% to 100%, how much can God act without affecting all people's free-choice? Should prayer override our choice to drive distracted or impaired? *Pause and digest — agree, disagree, or discuss?*
3. Less impact — Let's propose God *did* intervene to make it *less* of an accident, 'safer-*er* travels' by helping you slow down or observe some danger, did you give thanks to God?
4. Impossible to please — If God intervened 99.999% of the time without a scratch, including many 'near misses', are you impossible to please and demand God's perfect irritation-free performance? Did you give thanks to God for all those other 99.999% of 'safe travels'?
5. Future unseen — Did that little car accident save you from a worse event just one block later? We'll never know on earth. Only God knows.
6. The system runs — God has instituted physical laws that continue to function without his intervention; gravity, fog, bugs, freezing. Were you respecting God's systems as they function to *prevent* an accident?
7. . . . insert yours here . . .

Should we pray for 'safe travels' or 'healing' or *anything*? Yes, absolutely yes. In fact, this author feels we should pray for *everything*,

---

[33] 2 Corinthians 4:18 "So we fix our eyes not on what is seen, but on what is unseen. For what is seen is temporary, but what is unseen is eternal."

[34] 2 Corinthians 12:8 "Three times I pleaded with the Lord to take it away from me."

ceaselessly,[35] because even if our hearts are wrong in our asks, our minds are being enlightened (literally 'light placed in') when we pray, helping us learn to be more in-tune with Him.

Praying for God's peace and righteousness[36] in a circumstance *can also help* our prayers come true. Praying for 'safe travels' helps us focus and take steps for exactly that — 'safe travels'. *Pause and digest — agree, disagree, or discuss?*

Arguments Against

But... But... But... For some, the above line of reasoning is hollow, or worse, flim-flam. The real problem in believing in the loving, miraculous relationship with God, Jesus Christ, and the Holy Spirit is... *our mindset*. If 1,000 amazing wonderful things happen, humans can get locked-in and focus on the *single miniscule unpleasant thing*. For them, *nothing* is good enough but a smooth life filled with pillows and cupcakes (for *that* we will have to wait to leave this world![37]).

We HATE it when bad things happen (especially *to us*). But we need to change this mindset habit (metanoeó 3340) of focusing on the bad. Instead focus on our *overwhelming* blessings heaped upon blessings from God.[38]

Here are some things you may have never thanked God for that are blessings:
- Dealing with difficult people
- Toilet paper
- Air conditioning
- Those things you don't like about yourself that actually served you well
- Shoes
- Soft pillows
- A tongue
- ... insert yours here ...

---

[35] 1 Thessalonians 5:17 "Pray without ceasing."

[36] 2 Timothy 2:22 "Flee from youthful passions and pursue righteousness, faith, love, and peace, together with those who call on the Lord out of a pure heart."

[37] Revelation 21:4 "'He will wipe away every tear from their eyes,' and there will be no more death or mourning or crying or pain, for the former things have passed away."

[38] Matthew 6:33 "But seek first the kingdom of God and His righteousness, and all these things will be added unto you."

But... But... But... What if the Church prays for healing and the person passes on to Heaven? Is this God's 'punishment' or 'for your good'?[39] Heavens no!

God is Love! God loves You! God loves *them*! Jesus and the Holy Spirit are proof! Prayer is about a mindset exchange for our correction and growth *for eternity*. Punishment or causing pain does *not* help us grow stronger in the love of Jesus Christ. Putting darkness on God when He is *only light*[40] misrepresents God.

Physical things happen and will continue to happen (free-choice and physics) on this earth.[41] God does not *cause* everything (allowing it is different than causing it). Humans cause a lot of our own grief. The Liar wants you to believe God is filled with darkness, causing bad things, to separate you from the *love of the God*.[42]

God, Jesus, and the Holy Spirit are with you to help[43] you *through* everything *and* the person you are praying for. God does not cure every physical issue. He cures all our *spiritual* issues.[44]

Why pray? Pray to acknowledge God's presence, the God that brought us *to Himself* through Jesus Christ and *resides in us* as the Holy Spirit, all to fulfill our need of a relationship *with Him*.[45]

Pray always.[46] Union. Mature. Share.

How Does This Apply?

God loves you: Remember this always
Union in Prayer: So you can be in Him
Mature in Prayer: Share His heart, mind, and strength
Share in Prayer: His love to others.

---

[39] 1 John 4:18 "There is no fear in love, but perfect love drives out fear, because fear involves punishment. The one who fears has not been perfected in love."

[40] 1 John 1:5 "And this is the message we have heard from Him and announce to you: God is light, and in Him there is no darkness at all."

[41] Ecclesiastes 11:3 "If the clouds are full, they will pour out rain upon the earth; whether a tree falls to the south or to the north, in the place where it falls, there it will lie."

[42] Romans 8:39 "... nor height nor depth, nor anything else in all creation, will be able to separate us from the love of God in Christ Jesus our Lord."

[43] Psalm 121:2 "My help comes from the LORD, the Maker of heaven and earth."

[44] 2 Corinthians 4:16 "Therefore we do not lose heart. Though our outer self is wasting away, yet our inner self is being renewed day by day."

[45] Hebrews 4:16 "Let us then approach the throne of grace with confidence, so that we may receive mercy and find grace to help us in our time of need."

[46] Luke 18:1 "Then Jesus told them a parable about their need to pray at all times and not lose heart: ..."

22. Repent, Metanoeó 3340[1]

Culture has smeared Christianhood with guilt, shame, and pain, but Jesus never did those things! If we know Jesus, we know the Father, so He can't be after your guilt, shame, and pain either.[2] Did you hear that? God is <u>not into punishing</u> you, no matter what you do or don't do.[3] That is a do-do trap! He's covered your not-love acts. He isn't going to the cross again.[4] It is <u>finished</u>. What then is the root of this dark smear on His love?

What does 'repent' mean?

▲   ▲
'Pent' again   'Sorry'

High Level

You can't 'pent' again since 'pent' is not even a word. And 'sorry'? Sorry for getting *caught*? Sorry the victim got mad? Or sorry for the not-love? No, 'sorry' by itself is too vague.

'Repent' was chosen during the 1300's European culture, which took the Latin word 'poena' (guilt, shame, and pain) and gave birth to a multitude of oppressive words: 'repent', 'penance', and 'penalty'. But the English chose the wrong word to understand the Greek.

The English chose 'repent' for the Greek word 'metanoeó'. Metanoeó is literally 'changed mind', implying our mind changed to God's. It is a combination of 'meta' (3326 <u>changed</u> [also: with, new, next, after, beyond]) as in '<u>meta</u>-morphosis' (*changed*-form), plus 'noeó' (3539 <u>mind</u> [also: understanding, thought]) as in 'para-<u>noia</u>' (irregular-*mind*). The Hebrew version of metanoeó is "שׁוּב" (shoob

---

[1] Metanoia 3341 is the noun (repentance), 3340 metanoeó is the verb (repent).

[2] You wouldn't do that to your children, and neither does God. Matthew 7:11 "So if you who are evil know how to give good gifts to your children, how much more will your Father in heaven give good things to those who ask Him!"

[3] Note that "discipline" is to educate, *very* different than punish. The only painful scourging ("chastise") is <u>our</u> pride and flesh that is removed to accept <u>His</u> lordship and <u>His</u> mastery in our lives. Hebrews 12:6 "For the Lord disciplines the one He loves, and He chastises every son He receives." Learning is from God; pain is from man.

[4] Romans 6:9 "For we know that since Christ was raised from the dead, He cannot die again; death no longer has dominion over Him."

H7725) also meaning 'turn your mind to God's ways' — validation that 'changed mind' is the right meaning since it is consistent with God's message to us in both Old and New Testaments.

> **Repent; μετανοέω; metanoeó:**
> Strong's 3340. To think different after, a *profound* change.

John the Baptist's message of 'repent' from your 'sin'[5] would be understood in his time as 'turn to God' from 'missing the mark', or as this author puts his definition of 'repent' here: 'change your mind to God's from your own not-love'.

This author is not so presumptuous to state he knows *which specific* flavor of these definitions were intended in the Bible in each of the 50+ times the Greek metanoeó based words (3340 'repent' and 3341 'repentance') were used, but it is clear that John the Baptist (in Hebrew, Greek, or Aramaic) was warning the religious people to stop making up a fake God of 'religious works' and turn to the *real God* of love, compassion, and mercy.[6] *Pause and digest — agree, disagree, or discuss?*

And that is the point of this chapter:

Christian! Stop Putting Guilt, Shame, and Pain into Your Relationship with God!

Why? Because you can't be victorious like that! If your relationship with God is filled with guilt and shame, you are under the heel of the Snake, when it is <u>YOU</u> who are supposed to be crushing *him*![7]

There is no guilt, shame, and pain with God in the new Jerusalem[8] — which means there should be <u>none</u> in our relationship with God <u>now</u>.

Do we think and act in not-love ways today? Absolutely — and there is allowance for that — but there is no excuse to *pursue* or *grow* those not-love habits. There is allowance for it to occur because Jesus knew that you were going to do it and He still loves you! But we have to press on to the goal,[9] which is maturity in Him. Jesus *wants* you to

---

[5] Mark 1:4 "John the Baptist appeared in the wilderness, preaching a baptism of repentance for the forgiveness of sins."

[6] Mark 1:15 "'The time is fulfilled,' He said, 'and the kingdom of God is near. Repent and believe in the gospel!'"

[7] Romans 16:20 "The God of peace will soon crush Satan under your feet. The grace of our Lord Jesus Christ be with you."

[8] Revelation 21:4 "'He will wipe away every tear from their eyes,' and there will be no more death or mourning or crying or pain, for the former things have passed away."

[9] Philippians 3:14 "I press on toward the goal to win the prize of God's heavenly calling in Christ Jesus."

mature more in Him as His representative of love here on earth. Learning God's love for you is the *source* of that maturing.

All metanoeó (changed mind) depends on *knowing* God's love for you — not hearing about it or being taught it — *knowing it* every day and every moment. Knowing it is a lifetime journey. How can this book teach everything to you so that you can *know* God's love for you? It can't but it can try. And even still this book won't be written 'right' since a year from now we'll all be in a different place *knowing* God's love for us.

God's love for us is the cause of our changed mind and resultant 'new' self. Our actions should result from gratitude and thankfulness for His love instead of guilt, fear, or obligation ("I want God to be pleased with me" [God *already is* pleased with you[10]] or "I don't want to make God mad" [God *doesn't get mad at you* since you are His child trying to learn]). These sources for our actions, gratitude versus guilt, are totally different. It is a *nuance* but a very important one to check so that we don't fall into the guilt driven do-do trap, instead staying in the guilt-free love of God. Just the fact that you *can* know God's love for you — how amazing!

Still, we won't be perfect. When you do not-love things in this world, own it, try to fix what was done wrong, ask God how to prevent it, learn, and move on to being more mature.[11]

The Parable of the Toad

Did you know that toads can drown? Really. (No, this author isn't getting distracted.) You too were once a tadpole, swimming in the dark, surrounded by water. "Dark? Water? Where?" asks the tadpole. It doesn't know that it is, for the tadpole life just *is*.

But then — above — it sees a light. It is drawn to the light. Things begin to change inside the tadpole. One day, by choice or inevitable transition, the tadpole is transformed! It is reborn on land as a toad. Only *now* does it know what darkness is. Only *now* does it know the lightness of breathing *air*. The toad is free!

And here is the kicker — the toad can never go back to being a tadpole! It may think it is a tadpole. It may try to do the things a tadpole

---

[10] Zephaniah 3:17 "The LORD your God is among you; He is mighty to save. He will rejoice over you with gladness; He will quiet you with His love; He will rejoice over you with singing."

[11] John 5:14 "After these things Jesus finds him in the temple and said to him, 'Behold, you have become well. [Miss the mark] no more, that something worse should not happen to you.'"

used to do. But it is *not* a tadpole and will *never again* be a tadpole. It is a toad. And if it pursues its old way of life, the toad could drown, it could die. The toad may make mistakes, but the toad's path to success is to have a changed mind and live as God intended the toad to be!

This would be the time where one of the disciples in the New Testament would ask Jesus, "Rabbi, what does *this* mean? The parable means this: You accepted Christ. You are transformed. Accept this. Grow into the *who* God intended *you to be!*[12]

Does Metanoeó Fit the Trinity + You Plan?

Who changes you? Jesus or you? If you could do it yourself, you would! We must recognize that Jesus is the author and finisher[13] of our journey with Him, which is why we need to stop do-do-doing, stop the toiling, and rest in Jesus.[14]

You and your works aren't the most important — *He is*! Put Jesus on top! You don't make *you* 'better' — *He does*![15] It is up to you to ask, listen, and submit to being led by Jesus[16] into a changed mind, metanoeó, *His* mind, *that* is what will make you better![17] *Pause and digest — agree, disagree, or discuss?*

The Holy Spirit is with us to help us because God loves us. He can work to heal us each day and through the decades in our submission, but we have free-choice to choose our actions every moment, every hour, every day. God won't choose for us. He supports us, He *understands* our pain, but we have free-choice to choose where and how we direct our heart and minds — thought, time, and effort, directed to the light or the dark.

---

[12] Philippians 3:13 "Brothers, I do not consider myself yet to have taken hold of it. But one thing I do: Forgetting what is behind and straining toward what is ahead, . . ."

[13] Hebrews 12:2 "Let us fix our eyes on Jesus, the author and perfecter of our faith, who for the joy set before Him endured the cross, scorning its shame, and sat down at the right hand of the throne of God."

[14] Matthew 11:28 "Come to Me, all those toiling and being burdened, and I will give you rest."

[15] Ephesians 2:8 "For it is by grace you have been saved through faith, and this not from yourselves; it is the gift of God, . . ."

[16] Psalm 139:10 ". . . even there Your hand will guide me; Your right hand will hold me fast."

[17] Acts 26:20 "First to those in Damascus and Jerusalem, then to everyone in the region of Judea, and then to the Gentiles, I declared that they should [change their minds (metanoeó 3340)] and turn to God, performing deeds worthy of their [changed mind (metanoia 3341)]."

Does a good tree bare bad fruit?[18] Are you one of God's children with the Holy Spirit in you? As you yearn (heart), as you think (mind), as you choose (free-choice), so goes your life.[19]

In your need, reach for Jesus through the Holy Spirit. You still will produce not-love thoughts, words, or deeds, though as you are able, *keep reaching for Jesus*. God understands when not-love happens, but there is *no excuse to pursue it*.

How does a changed mind (metanoeó) occur? Pursue Jesus, live in the Trinity + You union, every moment, every hour, of every day.

Test It

How are you more *powerful* in Christ:
- In a state of guilt, shame, and pain, or
- love, compassion[20] and mercy?

What will produce the most *fruit* in Christ:
- A relationship squeezed off by fear[21] or
- filled with the full flow of Jesus's love?

Pause and digest — agree, disagree, or discuss?

Jesus taught that *people* are mean to other *people* in this physical world, and we need *His changed mind* (metanoeó) *now* to live spiritually for eternity.[22]

He also taught that regardless of our 'goodness', natural disasters can happen to us in this physical world, and it is <u>not</u> because of what you did![23] Regardless of our physical focus, again, it is *His changed*

---

[18] Matthew 7:18 "A good tree cannot bear bad fruit, and a bad tree cannot bear good fruit."

[19] Galatians 6:7 "Do not be deceived: God is not to be mocked. Whatever a man sows, he will reap in return."

[20] Mark 1:41 "Moved with compassion, Jesus reached out His hand and touched the man. 'I am willing,' He said. 'Be clean!'"

[21] Mark 4:19 "... but the worries of this life, the deceitfulness of wealth, and the desire for other things come in and choke the word, and it becomes unfruitful."

[22] Luke 13:2 "To this He replied, 'Do you think that these Galileans were worse sinners than all the other Galileans, because they suffered this way?'"

[23] Luke 13:4 "Or those eighteen who were killed when the tower of Siloam collapsed on them: Do you think that they were more sinful than all the others living in Jerusalem?"

mind (metanoeó) *in us (Trinity + You)* that makes the difference in our life now and forever.[24]

Takeaway

Bad stuff happens, and most of it is due to mankind, so don't let the Liar smear God's good name. We need God to make this world good, and He can through us!

God is Love. When in doubt, pray, test it, and dig deeper. Keep reaching for God's true Word — *Himself*.[25]

God is Love,
Submit to God, so that
Your mind can be changed to God's
To love others as you and they are able
As He loves you.

---

[24] Acts 11:18 "And having heard these things, they were silent and glorified God, saying, 'Then indeed God has given also to the Gentiles [changed mind (metanoia 3341)] unto life.'"

[25] Matthew 20:33 "'Lord,' they answered, 'let our eyes be opened.'"

23. Faith, Pistis 4102

You see the word 'faith' everywhere, but should it be? Is faith 'belief' or more than that? What is the purpose of faith? Where does it come from — all from God or all from yourself?

Where does faith come from?

▲ 100% from You   ▲ 100% from God

High Level

The answer is both. Faith is both from you and God. Faith is the *quantity* of *union* with God. Faith *strengthens* God's plan: life is for a relationship with *Him*.

Faith is a *substance*. Faith is a *thing*. What kind of 'thing'? Faith is a 'thing' you can *trust* that *secures the relationship*, like ties, ropes or cables attached to rock, *things* that provide assurance and conviction, just as the Bible says:

Now faith is the assurance of things hoped for, the conviction of things not being seen. —Hebrews 11:1

It is *not* belief. Faith is beyond *hopeful belief* to *actual* <u>trust</u>. Demons 'believe' but do not act *trusting* Jesus Christ.[1]

Faith implies reliance, not approval. Faith is trusting in something we can rely on, anchored on God's rock, a rock that exists regardless of our beliefs *or approvals* of God's design. It is not anchoring our belief in *sand* — the Liar's fake god. Nor is it what we *make up* about God, or what *people* teach about God, faith must *be in* God. In Truth.

We have to know *in Whom* we have faith[2] (not faith in a few English words chosen from our Bible translation, but in Jesus Christ Himself). We then tie ourselves to that *Truth*, the *Him* that is *Truth*. The greater

---

[1] James 2:19 "You believe that God is one. You are doing well! Even the demons believe *that*, and shudder!"

[2] 2 Timothy 1:12 "For this reason, even though I suffer as I do, I am not ashamed; for I know whom I have believed, and I am convinced that He is able to guard what I have entrusted to Him for that day."

quantity of ties to the Truth — Jesus Christ — the greater is our 'faith' union and the juicier is the fruit produced from that Trinity + You union.

Union *with the Trinity* allows us to live in the righteousness *of the Trinity*.[3] Pause and digest — agree, disagree, or discuss?

Faith Across the Chasm

Let us imagine you are on one side of a chasm. Your friend wants to meet for lunch. You trust them to meet their promise, anchor yourself to them, act on it, and form a union with them. But would you trust them to take a bullet for you to save your life? Not likely. The *quantity* of union isn't that strong to trust that promise from a 'lunch friend'.

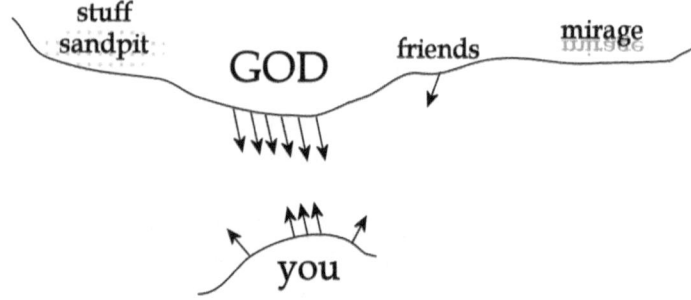

Similarly, people union to their money or stuff,[4] trusting these material things to anchor their current happiness and their eternity on. This is a union anchored on sand.[5]

Another misguided attachment is when the Liar tries to get you to attach to the Law, a mirage god that is completely worthless, off from the real God.[6] It looks right, but it is *all wrong*.[7] The Liar contradicts what God said and who God *is*.[8] We may even help the Liar, by creating our own false god by making the relationship do-do based: "If I do this, God will do that. . . ." But no one can anchor to lies.

---

[3] Romans 1:17 "For the gospel reveals the righteousness of God that comes by faith from start to finish, just as it is written: 'The righteous will live by faith.'"

[4] 1 Timothy 6:17 "Instruct those who are rich in the present age not to be conceited and not to put their hope in the uncertainty of wealth, but in God, who richly provides all things for us to enjoy."

[5] Matthew 7:26 "But everyone who hears these words of Mine and does not act on them is like a foolish man who built his house on sand."

[6] Romans 4:14 "For if those who live by the law are heirs, faith is useless and the promise is worthless, . . ."

[7] Matthew 4:1-11 and Luke 4:1-13, "The Temptation of Jesus"

[8] Genesis 3:4 "'You will not surely die,' the serpent told her."

One can only anchor to Truth, Jesus Christ, the author and finisher of our faith-union.[9] He is the house built on *rock*, the strong foundation planned by God.[10]

As we keep *adding* cables across the canyon, anchored to Jesus Christ, our faith-union grows stronger in *Him*, we understand better how to live in *Him*, the more in-synch we are in Him until His goodness permeates all areas of our life.[11] *Pause and digest — agree, disagree, or discuss?*

It is God's designed life path for us to mature in His Spirit. By creating a greater faith-union, we learn not to see with our physical eyes, but to see with His heart of love in us. By living in-tune with God, Jesus, and the Holy Spirit, we realize more and more that God's physical world runs with unseen spiritual things[12] — like souls, love, and relationships. The greater quantity of ties across the chasm, anchoring us solidly to God, the more we flow out His goodness (love) in this world.

> **Faith; καρδία; pistis:**
> Strong's 4102. Used 243 times. It means beliefs, support, trust, or reliance on God's thoughts.
>
> Beliefs not from God are not-God (Romans 14:23) no matter the size (Luke 16:10)!

Test It

Does faith anchor on Jesus Christ, the one who overcame death (in other words, <u>not</u> you)? True![13]

Has this *expanded* the definition of faith more than it should? Or, has this definition *limited* the power of God? *Pause and digest — agree, disagree, or discuss?*

What if we don't have this faith-union? We're not "of God" because we're not approaching *Him* to find out what *He* wants,[14] which means

---

[9] Hebrews 12:2 "Let us fix our eyes on Jesus, the author and perfecter of our faith, who for the joy set before Him endured the cross, scorning its shame, and sat down at the right hand of the throne of God."

[10] Hebrews 11:10 "For he was looking forward to the city with foundations, whose architect and builder is God."

[11] 1 Corinthians 1:5 "... that in everything you have been enriched in Him, in all speech and all knowledge, ..."

[12] Hebrews 11:3 "By faith we understand the universe to have been formed by *the* word of God, so that the things being seen have not been made from the things being visible."

[13] 1 John 5:5 "Now who is the *one* overcoming the world, except the *one* believing that Jesus is the Son of God?"

[14] Hebrews 11:6 "And without faith it is impossible to please God, because anyone

we are getting our 'ideas' from somewhere else (not God)! *Pause and digest — agree, disagree, or discuss?*

What about all those, "your faith" quotes in the Bible, aren't they from the believer?
1. "Your faith" may be indicating your "union". An easy check is to replace "faith" with "union". "Union" is a relationship, so the believer still needs to reach out, listen, submit, and act — doing our part — but it is *Him* we trust, not trust in ourselves.
2. The English "your faith" may also be a Greek translation of "THE faith" operating in you, which means it is Jesus working in you, *His* gift inside you, which you exercise.[15] Like 'your' rental car, it really isn't 'yours'. Or like 'your' eternal life which really isn't 'yours' either since it was made possible only by Jesus Christ. *Pause and digest — agree, disagree, or discuss?*

But really, where does 'faith' start, you or the Trinity? Do people have free choice or not? This author would reply that our little minds will never know for sure the entire Holy design until Heaven, and that arguing about it doesn't help us love God and love others *today*, so that this question doesn't matter since it doesn't help us *love more*. However, knowing that humans demand to know everything and keep trying to eat off the Tree of Knowledge, he will attempt to answer though he is open to other arguments.

The author answers thus: Faith starts from God, at birth, since He knew you and loved you in your womb from the beginning, writing His laws on your heart and planting his <u>little</u> seeds of love in you. The 'cables-across-the-chasm' from Him to us may be <u>little</u> or weak, but *He* has been there our whole lives talking to us and trying to get us to accept His love. When we finally accept Christ as our Savior, *accept* His gift of *relationship*, and *grab on* to His 'cables-across-the-chasm', the *quantity and strength* of the faith-cables-union grows. Those <u>little</u> mustard seeds of faith that *God* gave us in the beginning can grow into ginormous trees of faith as we reach out *to Him* to grow our faith-union relationship *in Him*.[16] Or one could relate our growing faith to His

---

who approaches Him must believe that He exists and that He rewards those who earnestly seek Him."

[15] Discussed further in *HELPS Word Studies* from the *Discovery Bible*. Examples given are: Matthew 9:2, 9:29; Luke 17:19; Philippians 2:17; 2 Peter 1:5.

[16] Matthew 13:31-32 "He put before them another parable, saying: 'The kingdom of the heavens is like a grain of mustard seed, which a man having taken, sowed in his field [God planted in us!], which indeed is smallest of all the seeds; but when it is grown, it is

parable of '*our* branch grows from *His* vine'. Regardless, this position that 'faith starts from God' meshes well with other parts of the Bible, where *He* is the source,[17] foundation, and beginning, and we, *when in union with Him*, are His outlet of love here on this earth, every moment anywhere and anytime, as the Trinity + You. *Pause and digest — agree, disagree, or discuss?*

Wrap It Up

Faith-union-quantity is the *substance and evidence* of things believed, the *security* from God, Jesus, and the Holy Spirt which you can trust to live,[18] the *provider* of peace from Jesus Christ, and something to nurture every day.

Or put another way:

Relationship with God, Jesus, and the Holy Spirit,
    leads to
Security in God, Jesus, and the Holy Spirit,
    leads to
Living from the union of God, Jesus, and the Holy Spirit + You.

---

greater than the garden plants, and becomes a tree, so that the birds of the air come and encamp in its branches [others may enjoy the love that God planted in us!].'"

[17] Acts 3:16 "By faith in the name of Jesus, this man whom you see and know has been made strong. It is Jesus' name and the faith that comes through Him that has given him this complete healing in your presence."

[18] 2 Corinthians 5:7 "For we walk by faith, not by sight."

24. Pneuma Transform

In math, for some difficult problems, converting 'unknown' items makes problems easier to solve. Specifically, performing a *Fourier Transform* converts the 'unknowns' into a new view. From this new view, the mathematician can then perform a *Fourier Analysis* to easily solve what was a difficult problem.

Likewise, in some difficult biblical problems, performing a *Pneuma Transform* converts 'unknown' items into a new view. From this new view, the disciple can then perform *Pneuma Analysis* to easily solve what was a difficult biblical problem.

Original Verse

For example, reading a shortened Matthew 21:21[1] Jesus says,

"If you have faith and don't doubt, if you say to this mountain, 'Be thrown into the sea,' it will happen."

Breaking down this verse from a standard physical view:
1. 'I' must produce the faith.
2. The faith must have <u>no</u> doubt.
3. <u>My</u> faith-created-power can do great physical things.

The standard physical view creates the following difficult problems:
1. Nobody moves physical mountains.
2. Where biblical disciples cured the sick,[2] we pray to heal the sick and they pass on to Heaven.
3. It is all <u>my</u> power and <u>my</u> fault, no God needed. All consequences are <u>my</u> weakness or 'faith doubts'. (scary!)

... And *this*(?!) creates desire for an eternal relationship, God and me? No way! The standard 'physical view' and problems it creates does not help today's Christian disciple mature in Christ.

---

[1] Matthew 21:21 "'Truly I tell you,' Jesus replied, 'if you have faith and do not doubt, not only will you do what was done to the fig tree, but even if you say to this mountain, "Be lifted up and thrown into the sea," it will happen.'"

[2] Luke 9:2 "And He sent them out to proclaim the kingdom of God and to heal the sick."

Pneuma Transformed Verse

Let us now apply the Pneuma Transform, making all things viewed spiritually. The new view of the verse is transformed to,

"If you have <u>God-union</u> ~~faith and don't doubt~~,[3] <u>if God empowers</u> you to say to this <u>spiritual obstacle</u> ~~mountain~~, 'Be thrown into the sea,' it will happen." (And open up a whole new view!)

Performing the Pneuma Analysis to see the new view results:
1. Spiritual God-union produces spiritual ability. (True!)
2. God can overcome any spiritual obstacle. (True!)
3. God can heal, break chains, and liberate us by tossing the obstacle into the bottom of the sea.[4] (True!)
4. With spiritual obstacles removed, our life is open to living from a whole new view. (True!)

... And I <u>do want</u> to spend eternity in relationship, God and me! (True!)

Test Everything

Good fruit test: Is this a correct application of the Pneuma Transform to these verses, or does it lead to bad answers?

To check, which produces the better fruit — the Physical view or the Pneuma view? Which is more loving? Which path is better, where God puts all the work on *your* shoulders,[5] when the Gospel is about putting it on Jesus and making your burden light?[6] Which *fits* better into life as we know it? *Pause and digest — agree, disagree, or discuss?*

Proof

What is the *proof* for using the Pneuma Transform?

Jesus tried to explain to people their need to have a Pneuma Transform. He confused people stuck in the physical view, saying things like, "No one can see the kingdom of God unless you are born

---

[3] "doubt" is the Greek diakrinó (1252), which has meanings of "to separate from". Faith (God-trust-union) can not be "separated" *from God*, making this 'pneuma transform' true.

[4] Micah 7:19 "He will again have compassion on us; He will vanquish our iniquities. You will cast out all our sins into the depths of the sea."

[5] Numbers 11:14 "I cannot carry all these people by myself; it is too burdensome for me."

[6] Matthew 11:30 "For My yoke is easy and My burden is light."

again."[7] And the people responded from the physical view, "But you can't! You can't get back in the womb!"[8]

The frequency that we see 'pneuma' in the bible is also proof of the importance of a Pneuma Transform. Spirit (pneuma 4151, used 383 times) is used about as often as Father (patér 3962, 418 times) and Son (huios 5207, 382 times). Depending on the context, pneuma can be God's Spirit (Holy Spirit[9]), or God's breath of life,[10] or what God gives inside us, that 'us' that will go live eternally with God[11] — all spirit focused.

Author confession: The 'Pneuma Transform' then is nothing new, but a sticky way to remember to live viewing from God's Pneuma, submitting yourself to see with the eyes of His Holy Spirit, the voice of Jesus put inside of you *to be your helper in the physical world.*

How Then?

How does this work in practice? Ask Him and listen (prayer) in order to union (faith) your mind to His (metanoeó 3340).

Prayer (proseuchomai 4336) is the combination of Greek words of 'exchanging thoughts' or 'interfacing minds'. Specifically, prayer is the *method* of how we exchange our thoughts with God's thoughts.

Faith (pistis 4102) is defined as 'reliance on God', or some say 'trust', but it is always *because of God*. It is not *us* 'claiming' or 'persuading ourselves' — which would then be 'faith' in ourselves! Faith-trust is always anchored *on God*, the *quantity of union* with God's thoughts, desires and power (great faith-union[12] or little faith-union[13]).

---

[7] John 3:3 "Jesus replied, 'Truly, truly, I tell you, no one can see the kingdom of God unless he is born again.'"

[8] John 3:4 "'How can a man be born when he is old?' Nicodemus asked. 'Can he enter his mother's womb a second time to be born?'"

[9] Matthew 3:11 "I baptize you with water for repentance, but after me will come One more powerful than I, whose sandals I am not worthy to carry. He will baptize you with the Holy Spirit and with fire."

[10] Revelation 11:11 "But after the three and a half days, the breath of life from God entered the two witnesses, and they stood on their feet, and great fear fell upon those who saw them."

[11] Acts 7:59 "While they were stoning him, Stephen appealed, 'Lord Jesus, receive my spirit.'"

[12] Matthew 15:28 "Then Jesus answering said to her, 'O woman, great *is* your faith. It shall be to you as you desire.' And her daughter was healed from that very hour."

[13] Matthew 8:26 "And He says to them, 'O *you* of little faith, Why are you afraid?' Then having arisen, He rebuked the winds and the sea, and there was a great calm."

Faith (God-union-quantity) is therefore tied to prayer (God-thoughts-exchange) — you can't have one without the other — to achieve our changed-mind transformation (metanoeó 3340).

Faith inside of *you* is from union to *Him*. To be more powerful in God, we need to be more *in union* with God's desires and His works, so that *His* desires are *our* desires[14] (not the other way around!).

What is the fruit of your union with God, Jesus, and the Holy Spirit?

". . . so that the name of our Lord Jesus will be glorified in you, and you in Him, according to the grace of our God and of the Lord Jesus Christ." (2 Thessalonians 1:12)

Our *own* beliefs, thoughts, and self-talk *do* have strength to affect our lives and others around us, so we must be careful of what they are and the time we give them. To be at our best, it is best to be in-tune with Jesus, so that with the infinite power of our infinite loving God, He can help us be 'in-tune' with Him while remove the 'mountainous' obstacles in our lives.

God's *spiritual* healing, *spiritual* chain-breaking,[15] and *spiritual* obstacle removing power <u>can fix many physical things</u>, though it can't fix all physical things all the time. If *every* prayer would be fulfilled *every* time exactly as we asked it, would that be good or bad? *Pause and digest — agree, disagree, or discuss?*

God's spiritual (pneuma) view focuses on our *eternal* relationship with Him, which matures our spirit and heart in His love.[16] *Humans'* focus is more often the *temporary* — the physical condition which makes us *blind to the Holy.*[17]

Taking God's direction, we also need to focus on our eternal spiritual (pneuma) relationship with Him, since only then do we realize <u>God alone</u> defines <u>you</u>. 'You' are not defined by the *physical* 'you'. 'You' are the *spiritual* 'you' *defined by God.*

---

[14] 2 Thessalonians 1:11 ". . . for which also we pray always for you, that He may count you worthy of the calling of our God, and He may fulfill every good pleasure of goodness and work of faith with power, . . ."

[15] Leviticus 26:13 "I am the LORD your God, who brought you out of the land of Egypt so that you would no longer be slaves to the Egyptians. I broke the bars of your yoke and enabled you to walk in uprightness."

[16] Matthew 10:28 "Do not be afraid of those who kill the body but cannot kill the soul. Instead, fear the One who can destroy both soul and body in hell."

[17] John 3:12 "If I have told you about earthly things and you do not believe, how will you believe if I tell you about heavenly things?"

When God alone defines you, you are free![18] Free from the shackles of what your family said and says you 'are', free from what the Liar says you 'are', or what physical things (age, sickness, abilities) try to define you. You are not defined by those things; you are God's child! God defines you. *God made you!* God loves you! And God is telling you *right now* how special you are to Him if only we *listen!*[19]

The more union we have with God, living in Christ, relying on the Holy Spirit, the more living water will flow into the fruit of our joined spirit.[20] *His* love, *His* peace, *His* joy, *His* patience, *His* kindness, *His* goodness, *His* faithfulness (trust-union fullness), *His* gentleness, and *His* self-control, all from *His* Spirit *to* ours *independent* of any *physical* condition.[21]

Prayer is the method (God-thought-exchange-method) for union with the Trinity.

Faith is the quantity (God-union-quantity) of the Trinity's mind shaping our mind.

By prayer and faith (God thought quantity) the Pneuma Transform shifts our physical view to the Trinity's Spirit view to solve difficult problems and *TRANSFORM US* (metanoeó 3340)!

When facing problems, rely on the Spirit — apply the Pneuma Transform. By God moving mountains, it can give your life a whole new view.

What is the Key Transform?

Prayer with God,
    transforms your mind about your
Identity to God, from God,
    which transforms you to
Trust God to empower you to
    let Him love others through you.

---

[18] John 8:36 "So if the Son sets you free, you will be free indeed."

[19] Luke 12:7 "And even the very hairs of your head are all numbered. So do not be afraid; you are worth more than many sparrows."

[20] 2 Corinthians 12:10 "That is why, for the sake of Christ, I delight in weaknesses, in insults, in hardships, in persecutions, in difficulties. For when I am weak, then I am strong."

[21] Philippians 4:11 "I am not saying this out of need, for I have learned to be content regardless of my circumstances."

25. Ok, Now What?

Jesus loves you.
Now go live like it.

About the Author

Emmanuel DeWeg is a Dutch pseudonym which means "God with us" "is the Way". Emmanuel ("God with us") is the name given to Jesus in Matthew 1:23 to fulfill the prophesy in Isaiah 7:14. DeWeg ("the Way") is God's plan for salvation through Jesus Christ (prophesied by Isaiah 30:21, proclaimed by Jesus in John 14:6, and used by the first Church in Acts 9:2).

The "author" is a disciple of Jesus Christ, without special title, trying to live best in this world through Him. He looks to God, His written word (the Bible), and God's disciples (the body of Christ) here on earth for guidance, as should any study group to settle all discussion. In other words, the answer to any debate should be, "What does God say about that and how do we apply it from *His love*?"

Like those cited by Jesus of "great faith" (Matthew 8:10 and Matthew 15:28) our goal is to be as His children, yield our hearts to God, and let *His righteousness* flow through unique us. There is no magic formula or specific action, since the Trinity + You is *unique*. Everything flows from that relationship.

God loves you. Now go and live like it.

For comments or contributions to this edition, free resources, or to subscribe to future release information, please go to the publisher's website: EmmanuelDeWeg.org

www.ingramcontent.com/pod-product-compliance
Lightning Source LLC
Chambersburg PA
CBHW060614080526
44585CB00013B/821